HOW TO

Fall
in Love

AN ATHEIST'S GUIDE TO
FALLING IN LOVE WITH GOD

A Real-Life Love Story

Written by

APRIL DEQUITO

The Memorare
Remember oh Most Gracious Virgin Mary
that never was it known that anyone
who fled to your protection,
implored your help, and sought your intercession
was left unaided, inspired by this confidence, I fly unto you,
O Virgin O Virgin, My mother,
To you do I come, before you I stand, sinful and sorrowful,
O Mother of the world incarnate, Despise not our petition,
But in thy mercy,
Hear and answer us. Amen

Prayer to St. Michael
St. Michael the Archangel, defend us in battle
Be our protection against the wickedness and snares of the devil
May God rebuke him, we humble pray,
Though thou O Prince of the heavenly host,
By the power of God, Cast into hell, Satan
and evil spirits that roam about the world,
seeking the ruin of souls. Amen

Guardian Angel Prayer
Angel of God, my Guardian dear,
to whom God's love, commits me here,
Ever this day, Be at my side
to Light and Guard, to Rule and Guide. Amen

CONTENTS

AUTHOR'S STATEMENT

I ask pardon for many editing oversights in this book. I did my best to have this book copy-edited as far as God would allow me. Upon my discernment, and as well as others who have tried to help in the editing of this book, God wants to maintain the authenticity of my narrative in its purest form, written primarily from my heart. As my friend would say, *"this book doesn't have to be perfect, and follow the rules of this world, because the world could never fathom the depth of God's love, and the wonder of my relationship with him. And it is through the imperfections, this book included, God's Perfect Love, can be made known to and felt by the readers"*

I dedicate this book for the continued *Healing, Conversion, Deliverance and Enlightenment* of my entire family, especially my *mother* - that they, too, will fall in love with God;

And more importantly, to **Mama Mary**, for always interceding for me, and whose love brought me closer to Jesus

ACKNOWLEDGMENT

I wish to acknowledge the following persons for their ideas and support, without whom, this book would not have been possible: *Danny*, my FB follower from Canada, who first encouraged me to write about my spiritual journey, and *Chin*, for the time you spent during my first attempt in writing this book. *Melissa Herbito*, who rekindled the idea of writing my book, my fellow book worm I met in the community park back in high school, and have been one of my very best friends that I truly value in my life. *Fr. Jose Españo*, my Spiritual Director, whose spiritual guidance have been instrumental in inspiring me to continue writing about my spiritual journey especially in times where I felt intimidated of exposing my life story in a book. *Fidel Bernados & Patchica Sevilla*, my fellow lay collaborators in the Archdiocese of Cebu Office of Deliverance & Exorcism (ACODE) & Alliance of the Holy Family International (AHFI), whose support in prayers have helped me in maintaining the courage to continue writing. *Elena Pedigo Clark*, one of my very good friends from International House, NY, where despite the distance and years apart, have significantly helped me get the resources on everything about publishing a book, from editing to final presentation, and whose encouragement kept on inspiring me to continue. *Jose Mari Zosa*, for his legal review and support on publishing, and keeping me on track. *Arnel Gaviola*, for sharing his publishing experience with me. *Trinidad Ybanez*, whose friendship helped me get my most needed feedback on areas of my life where I felt extremely vulnerable. *Charo Roncesvalles*, for your creativity, friendship, and fulfilling your promise to make my book cover should I decide to publish a book. *Fr. Peter Otsuji*, for your insights. *Milagros & Simeon Dumdum* for their daughter, and my best friend, *Simone*, whose love and friendship had been instrumental in my transformation and conversion. *For all the men* I have fallen in love with that led me to love God. And *for all the people*, friends & foes alike, that contributed to my transformation & conversion

And most importantly, to our ***Almighty God***, for authoring my life and for not allowing me to be separated from his saving grace. 🙏

INTRODUCTION

I love books. It's basically my only fetish where I find it difficult to leave, once I go inside a bookstore. Once I'm on a roll, I find myself stuck in a bookstore for hours until closing time. I don't necessarily read them all but I try to get the gist of what each book has to offer. There are still so many books I haven't read completely – not because they turned out to be awful but because I always tend to give myself time to grow into it. The difficult part is getting past the first chapter.

For as long as I can remember, it has always been a lifelong dream of mine to write a book. Most importantly, to write my story. But then I get so overwhelmed with all the things I want to talk about that I find it difficult to focus on one particular aspect of my life. So, I decided, I'll try out writing a blog instead. Since I rely on my mood, like most writers, I tend to write sporadically. My entries are oftentimes very long and spontaneous. I'd publish all in one sitting then I'd stop again. Usually in 3 years. My breaks usually take that much longer before I write again.

I like writing spontaneously. I find it liberating to do so, and that is why I mostly post diligently on my Facebook (FB) status. And so, every 3 years, I'd compile my FB status into a series of blogs.

The plan to publish was always there but I never truly considered it until I was approached by a stranger on my messenger who followed my posts that he felt, as compelled by God, to reach out to me and encourage me to publish a book about my spiritual journey. That was in 2023. He was pretty diligent on following me up and so I tried to look for people to help me. In my first attempt, I chose an editor who didn't really have any commercial experience in editing a book. I recalled he edited a virtual magazine about swimmers (I am an open water swimmer and that's how we met) and he also writes very well, with impeccable grammar and all, and so I thought maybe he would do. As we got closer to making it happen, he backed out because he felt that he may not be the right person because there were some aspects about the topic, I was planning to include in my book that he didn't agree with nor subscribe to. I couldn't even think of a title. A particular focus. I know I wanted to talk about God. And how much I love him. But I didn't know what the structure would be like. I found it too overwhelming.

The next thing I knew, I had placed the book plans in the back burner. One thing led to another – I got officially installed in the Ministry of Spiritual Liberation and Exorcism, and I got busy serving in the ministry. Being in this ministry has significantly fueled my spiritual growth in leaps and bounds. I have gone through years of "purification" during the pandemic, where I learned to entrust everything to

God. For a while, I have always practiced relying on divine providence even if I have my own business to run, and precisely because I run the business, I am responsible for my workers and their families. While I own the business, it would seem more like I am working for them than me working for me. I'm working and managing the company so I can pay their salaries and fulfill my obligations to my clients. I will talk more about this later in this book and how this impacts my spiritual life. I've mentioned this part of my life because lately, I couldn't seem to shrug off the anxiety in my heart. I keep on thinking of my business, my liabilities, and my future. This doesn't sound like I am entrusting things to God. But I do. Yet, the anxiety remained. I never stopped with my daily spiritual routine and I regularly examine my conscience. And I constantly serve everyone my Spiritual Director would ask me to help. I would spend over one hour in the Blessed Sacrament daily and for days, I have asked the Lord – *"Please speak to my heart Lord on what you want me to do. I don't know what it is that I haven't done or am not doing. Please speak directly to my heart Lord."*

Then one fine day, an old high school friend of mine, Melissa, called me up regarding her career move and as we settled hers, she was so kind enough to ask me about my career situation. Initially, we talked about what a good idea it is to probably start a Business Processing Outsourcing (BPO) business, and while we were discussing mutual friends doing business in the industry, we got around to a friend who was in the publishing business. Melissa told me, *"April, why don't you write your own book?!"* I was struck! That's where the idea of publishing a book was rekindled. After she said that, I felt a release in my heart and I knew, this is what God wants me to do. And it didn't just stop there. The title just blurted out of my mouth and the title felt good. Appropriate. Shortly after that, clients called me for a potential business endeavor. That is usually a telltale sign that God is giving me a treat because I got something right. Then, I hesitated. I started to procrastinate. I became anxious again. I felt a push. It's like God telling me, *"Move it April. Stop wasting time."*

I wanted to write a book for young adults because they are the ones that needed saving the most. Their generation. In a few years, they will become adults and they will be deciding on the fate of our country, the Philippines, or if not, the world. In this age of digital technology, where social media and artificial intelligence are now dictating how people think, we are simply running against time. Time. It's becoming a very scarce commodity.

Another reason why I want to target young adults is because they have more years in them, and they are still physically and mentally strong. One would ask, why does it matter when most people wait until they are old before they start looking for God? This is the mistake most people make. Spiritual warfare is the toughest fight man can ever do in his life. Most people will barely make it. Most people think getting ourselves into heaven is as simple as saying *"we believe."* The older one gets, depending on God's will, a person will not die without knowing the reality of God. Real accounts of famous last words of renowned atheists and even Protestants have been documented to have revealed the mistakes they made on their death bed. If one would take into account the life and death of the late Nobel-Laureat Awardee, George Price, a world-famous geneticist, who lived most of his life as an atheist and later converted to Roman Catholicism on the twilight of his life, one would think twice in delaying. If you are an unbeliever and you start doubting the possibility that there is a God, I suggest you take advantage of that even if you start off by faking it. It's better than not taking it into consideration at all. Only God knows if Price made it to heaven because in spite of his conversion and total sacrifice to pay for his offenses, and even going as far as giving up his entire material wealth, he ended up committing suicide. This is not to say that he didn't ask God for forgiveness before dying. I have my own testimony of this moment of recollection that God will give us, depending on his mercy- that we can always trust to be infinite.

Even the mistake most Catholics think that getting ourselves into heaven is as simple as going to church every Sunday. But those are just the bare minimum to help us navigate our way into imitating Christ. Most Catholics will go to confession once a year and think they don't have any sins anymore but when we process them, the list of unconfessed sins since childhood could fill up an entire page and more. Simply put, every sin comes with demons. One can find more information about the concept of sin in the *Catechism of the Catholic Church (CCC): Part three: 1852*.

It took me a very long time to realize that it is sin that separates us from God. I learned the hard way how sin wounds our relationship with God. Because humility is a crucial requirement to have before we engage in spiritual warfare, I was constantly tested so I can at least acquire a certain level of humility. Humility is critical for one to survive being part of this ministry. I'll talk more about some of my experiences in spiritual warfare in one of the chapters. In my effort to acquire a certain level of humility, I realized that in order to make a proper confession where we can truly be liberated from the spirits that comes with our sin, it is absolutely critical that we must be humble enough to be honest. Why? Because we need to acknowledge what we have done that offended God. When we hurt another person, we are actually hurting God himself. When we lie to ourselves, we are hurting God because we are like children willfully covering our ears so we won't hear our parents reprimanding us. What makes a confession good is our awareness of our actions, decisions, or even lack of action that allowed evil to penetrate our soul. Our awareness comes from our memories that will remind us of our past actions. When we are truly willing, which mean we are humble, the Holy Spirit can speak to us directly. This is the most crucial part of preparing for confession – the examination of our conscience. It's an examination because we are being tested how much of our sins are we truly willing to acknowledge. Other people would claim they will just confess directly to God, which is a very unsafe method. Outside the sacrament of confession, we are vulnerable. One doesn't realize that this sacrament requires one to battle evil – to battle the spirit of dishonesty. On our own, without the humility of hiding ourselves in the authority of Jesus, one can trust we won't ever stand a chance. I will describe later how this applies to me and how I discovered the *liberating* power of a good confession.

While our sins are forgiven during confession, as executed by a priest, who is "in Persona Christi" (Christ in person) but the wounds caused by our sins remain unhealed. It is critical that we offer *reparations* through suffering or personal transformation, and daily communion to repair the damaged caused by our sins with our relationship with God.

It is important to emphasize that we are the caretakers of Our self. There are two beings in a person. The "person" and the "self". The person refers to the body and the self refers to the soul. The person is subject to worldly distractions that we tend to forget the soul that is suffering inside of us. When we allow evil to penetrate our soul, our person will lose the wisdom that emanated from our soul through the guidance of the Holy Spirit. The person will start to listen to the voices of worldly attachments. A more in-depth explanation of this can be found in the *CCC: Part One: 362*

I will begin my story when I moved to New York City, with a letter I drafted for Paulo Coelho, as it genuinely described what "my thought process" was during that time and where I lost my faith completely, without realizing it. From the letter, you will realize how totally broken I am and how my entire motivation of moving to New York City was fundamentally driven by pride and sheer arrogance that I could all do it on my own. In that letter you will see how I have convinced myself that those voices were all just *mine*, but you will also see that there is that invisible hand guiding me. That letter demonstrated how at that particular moment of time, I never acknowledged the concept of God. I talked about the universe but never about God. I thanked Paulo Coelho for inspiring me but I was totally oblivious of God. I recall writing it with a conscious decision not to include God in the equation. In that letter, I emphasized that my personal legend was "finding myself." Well, there is nothing wrong with finding oneself. In fact, in order for us to find God, it is also critical for us to find ourselves. This letter truly demonstrated my sheer realization about my acceptance of myself, simply as I am, without having to apologize for what I truly am that makes me - Me.

I will take you back to my childhood, my background and my relationship with my father, who was an atheists and later attempted to start his own religion with me. A religion that is more human-centered *panthro* and god, at the same time - *theist*; and how his spiritual influence in me has gradually penetrated my psyche and the moment I got to New York city, far away from the spiritual protection of Cebu – my hometown surrounded by devout Catholics. I was easily met with deceptions that was increasing my separation from God. This is where I got involved with a psychic. I'll talk about my expulsion from my Master's Program, the injustice I experienced, the lawsuit I filed, and how these events in my life have significantly cornered me into letting evil enter my life. While at the same time, at the peak of my utter destruction, God saved me, only to realize that those events were all just God's way of bringing me home. And I'm sure you are thinking, *What? Why? How?* What if I tell you these "evil events" that God allowed to happen to me are sheer proof at how **extremely** romantic God is? A story wouldn't be romantic if there is no **heartache,** right? It wouldn't be romantic if there is no loss and feelings of hopelessness, right? And **tragedy** would be considered a significant expression of romance because many would claim it's a more authentic depiction of reality. But I wasn't one of those people. I only wanted to be happy. I was an idealist and I am only willing to accept a happy ending. I will tackle later where **my wants** are stemming from. One would be surprised to realize that these desires didn't come from the books I've read but it has a spiritual source that actual stems from demonic influence. I will talk more in detail about that.

I will also talk about my family – my conflict with them, how my relationship with them shaped my personality and behaviors based on the decisions I made, along with various conflicts I have been involved with all throughout my life. Very costly ones. I will be as authentic as I can be. A sinner. A hard core one. I will talk about my cruelty. My capacity to hurt people. My brokenness. My anguish. My purification. My liberation. My continued struggle. My spiritual awakening.

I will talk about my non-profit and how, in spite of its atheist undertones, helped me got home — and by home, back to God. I'll walk you thru from the moment I realized I have become an atheist, how I pretended to have faith, and the struggle I had to go thru to get it back. I'll narrate how I got it back and how it fueled my desire to engage in spiritual warfare, who I made an army with, and how I executed it. I will talk about the fruits and consequence of such endeavor and how it almost killed me. I'll talk about my involvement in the *Ministry of Spiritual Liberation*. I'll talk about how God healed me. I'll even talk how I first became aware of the reality of demons and how they attack me.

I will share about some dark moments. Very dark ones. I'll also be transparent about how I overcame pornography. Why is this relevant? Because a lot of people tend to downplay the extent to which pornography damages our soul, and the speed of it to significantly widen one's door to the demonic and not be able to notice it. Pornography significantly empowers the spirit of lust and vanity, both of which are very hard to resist because they are "pleasurable" sins — sins that ultimately deceive us to feel good, good that only refers to physical pleasures that are fleeting and temporary.

I'll walk you thru about my Near-Death Experience (NDE) or Out of Body Experience (OBE) where my soul separated from my body while attempting to finish a 70.3-mile Triathlon race in Da Nang, Vietnam and its pivotal role in my passion to continually transform as if I am running out of time.

I'll talk about my romantic life and how each of those romantic experiences were actually necessary for me to realize how I have fallen in love with God. I'll talk about my heartaches. How I dealt with them and how my last heartache has completely opened my heart to the Lord. I have always been into romance. My reading habit started back when I was in grade school. It was summer time and I borrowed my sister's novel, the Sweet Dreams Collection, just for show. Then I got attention from my neighbors, who got impressed that I was reading a novel already. I wasn't. But one day, I was gifted a book entitled, "*A Little Princess*" by Frances Hodgson Burnett. My brother read it and told me the story. I thought it sounded interesting so I tried reading it. It was the book that broke me and since then, I have been addicted. And since the books available to me were from my sister, I got hooked on romantic novels. My sister and I would go on a used-book store in Magallanes Street; one of the oldest streets in the Philippines, and would regularly trade in our books there. I would spend an entire summer just inside the house, reading. I would get so lost in the books. My father would indulge me because it assured him that I'll always be safe in the house for as long as I have books to read. These novels shaped my desire for romance. Now a days, people would find these authors as archaic- "Old school" as they say. The authors' writing style also significantly influenced mine as well. These novels also introduced me to soft porn.

Although these books emphasized on finding the **One**, but I learned the mystery of the *bees and the birds* from these novels too. Later, when I was introduced to the internet by my college friend Cathy, whose boyfriend back then was a computer wizard. My addiction for reading books dwindled though my desire to acquire books remained. I just don't read them anymore. I just loved collecting them.

This is truly a love story. A love story that you may have never heard written in this manner before. I hope that after reading this book, you will realize how God has been courting your heart for the longest time. All you have to do is to be **Open**. You don't need to force yourself to believe. Just be **Open**.

May you allow the *Holy Spirit* to speak to your heart as you read this book and know that I am writing this book from the standpoint of someone who is in love. I am writing this book because I am in love and hope you will feel that love as well reverberating to the very core of your being.

Are you ready? Sit back and enjoy reading.

A LETTER TO PAULO COELHO

Dear Paulo Coelho,

I read your book in 2003, about a year before I left for New York. The timing couldn't have been perfect. I embarked on a quest to find myself in New York City and brave the fear as Santiago did. I left everything behind to search for my personal legend, trusting that "indeed" the universe will conspire. *Trust* is such a big word. Trusting someone has never been my strongest trait yet I took the risk of trusting the universe.

Although, I know the book was written as a metaphor, I did believe it in my heart. The struggle was indeed painful and excruciating but what helped kept me going among many other inspirations I tried to seek was the thought of Santiago. What prevented me from coming home was "shame" – Shame of being called a failure. In many ways, I justified the experience by thinking of Santiago, that the search always entails sacrifices and suffering. Somewhere along the way, when I thought I was almost there, suddenly, everything that I worked so hard for were stripped away from me, coincidentally, similar to how Santiago lost everything he had because he was duped and later when he thought he was going nowhere with his journey.

When this happened to me, I have to admit (a big part of myself wanted to blame the book- so strongly). I questioned why did I allow myself to be placed in this situation? why did I leave the security of my own home when I had everything there? when I thought I've hit a brick wall, alone and helpless in a city so big as New York; when I thought I was defeated and that there's nothing I can ever do to alter the misery and the failure I was facing, I realized an opportunity; a calling – a whisper. It's like the universe was speaking to me. Some people may call it hallucination – but it wasn't. Because I've never felt this feeling of certainty in my life, wherein my fears are suddenly irrelevant. Because everything I feared would happen, already happened. In fact, much worse than what I imagined it to be. I could hear the voice within me so clearly now. I'm not sure how to explain it but having that feeling of certainty despite the uncertainty is just so liberating.

Everything I envisioned is so clear and exactly what I have been getting. I have learned to let go of things I felt I was entitled to without feeling begrudged. Everything I imagined happened exactly how I imagined it; in fact, even more. I started to account for the things or areas where I thought I made a mistake, and wondered how I could have changed them? And yet a voice within me would speak so loudly and say, "No! all the choices you made were exactly what you wanted," or thought I wanted. This realization made me realize how strong I have been that in times of distress and confusion, it was my deeds decisions, and trust in myself that pulled me back to face reality. The failure or the injustice, although painful, have made me see the vulnerability of being human. And yet, the lessons were significant. The people I've met because of this quest were unbelievably priceless and also made me see the beauty of being human. Along the way, I have met different kinds of people; shared different kinds of experiences that I would never have known or realized had I not left. These experiences, I will never trade for anything. My personal legend is the person I have become today. I have learned to finally acknowledge that voice - that was constantly there but I chose to ignore because I didn't trust it. A voice that I often disregard because other voices seemed to sound better. A voice that I often suppress because it doesn't seem to sound good to others even if it sounded perfectly well to me. My personal legend is finding the strength to finally be honest with myself. The struggle was well worth it. I know that the struggle will never end, and that there will be more battles to fight. But I also know and trust that for as long as I listen to that voice within me, guided by something cosmic, I can transform that struggle into an opportunity.

Thank you, Mr. Coelho - for your creativity have personified *life*; have helped me see or realize the faces of the different actors that one faces in one's life. The characters in your book pretty much covered the different spectrum of humanity. I don't know if this was your intention or if "*The Alchemist*" was just a mere story that you thought of writing with no particular purpose but entertainment. It wasn't just a story to me. It is indeed a metaphor of life's journey to finding oneself.

REDEMPTIVE ADVERSITY

I wrote this on my blog back in 2008 and published it in 2013. This part of my blog is practically the reason why I started writing because I wanted to heal. It took me several times revising it until I have reached a point that I felt justified by it. I also had to write it because back in 2016, I got involved in a cyber conflict where strangers would Google my name and find my US Court case that I filed against my university in New York City. People tend to not read on the details of the case and since I lost in that lawsuit - people would simply judge that I was guilty even if I was the complainant. Since it was such a traumatizing experience for me back then, and when people ask me about it, I find it so stressful to do so because it was such a long, complicated story. My mother's friend would simply summarize that I was being "maldita"- a Filipino term of someone who snaps and is prideful. While there is a lot of truth to it, the story goes much deeper than just about my behavior. I decided to write about it on a blog so that when somebody ask about it? I will just send them the link to my blog.

Similarly, I will include the full text (*with some redactions to exclude their real names and other unnecessary statements I made about them that is no longer relevant to the objective of this book*) from my blog below so I can demonstrate the authentic nature of how I was back when I was still clawing my way back to God.

Redemption

As I look into the horizon, I see the sea
So still, so empty, so endless
Beneath the deep blue waters
I see walls of ocean rocks
So deep, so dark, so rough

I looked at the dusk sky
So quiet, so misty, just watching
Who's out there? I yelled

Silence. Where am I?

Silence.

Thudding, I hear my heart beat in my ears
So fast, so painful, so heavy
Fear, darkness, panic
Wake up, wake up!

I am awake
It wasn't a dream
No, no!
It has to be!

I looked back
Islands, so many of them
Where am I?
In an island
Am I alone?

A breeze, a kiss of the wind
On the dusk sky, I see rays
So light, so thin, so bright
Further, further
Birds flying, beautiful patterns

My gaze dropped
Thick white fog,
Forms the horizon
Oh wait, a boat floating!
Redemption!
I just have to swim to it

Most people would wait until they are nearing their deathbeds before writing their life's memoir. They would wait until they are famous or infamous at a global scale. When I read about their lives, their experiences seem inapplicable to mine. I tried to emulate some of them- at least the ones I admire and the way they lived their lives but it just doesn't come out right. I decided to write a quarter-life memoir to free myself from whatever it is that is holding me back – *social crucifixion*.

I can only imagine how modern-day academics would rate my writing style, as they abhor any form of writing associated with any religious terms unless I can back it up with complicated high-sounding analytical terminology yet they would insist on keeping things simple without requiring them to think- at least that's what my thesis advisor claimed.

My writing was initially driven by my fall from grace that happened a few years ago. In my previous blogs, I have hinted an injustice done by certain faculty members. If one would search my name on google or any search engine, one could see a US court decision of an appellant (myself) suing a university. Yes! that would be me - an ordinary Cebuana suing a private University in New York City. And no, I did not win. Just to cut to the chase. I knew that I wouldn't win but the lawsuit was initially intended to re-instate me back to my program that I paid in full over the three years I've resided in New York city. The intention was for the University to hold my thesis advisor accountable for unethical behavior. Instead, the university chose to fight me in court. *Voilà!* What a surprise. Normally, people would back out and let things be. Let injustice be. Go back and hide in one's hole and pretend nothing bad ever happened. But I'm not a normal person and so is my father. I thank God every day for giving me a father that love me beyond recognition. I especially mentioned my father because the decision was not supported by the rest of my family for many practical reasons. Practicality often times get in the way of justice. People who experience injustice are not normal anymore. Injustice changes people whether for the better or for the worst. In my case, I would like to think that my decisions after have transformed me into someone better than I used to be.

I will further discuss the content of my thesis later, as my thesis eventually became one of my anchors and sources of inspiration that helped me kept my sanity or my will to live. Sounds fatalistic? It was. Having said that, for practical people not directly associated with academia, or for people living in poverty, this "so-called" disgrace would seem futile compared to the horrors they face in their everyday lives. I have that awareness but why did it still hurt? There are a lot of things in my life where I would feel I am terribly blessed but why did that particular experience shook me in ways that I felt there was no more light at the end of the tunnel? I'll tell you why.

Omnilogical Resource Pavilion (ORP):
The Master's Thesis

My master's thesis actually began during my undergraduate years in University of San Carlos (USC). It was originally my bachelor's thesis but I was discouraged then by our department dean as she thought the topic was too deep for me. My thesis advisor at that time also discouraged me because he thought my topic was too deep for the panelists to grasp.

The ORP was initially a multi-dimensional library and research facility that would study all fields of study. Obviously, I will need to know about psychology, which I didn't have any credits on. I did have sociology but I knew I needed to study more about it. I also needed to learn more about human evolution and anthropology. My plan was to program new kinds of spaces that study and educate people. It's going to be an elaborate research laboratory after all. I actually just adopted an original idea that my father coined himself. The word, Omnilogy, was actually my father's coinage. In my website and my paper, I didn't acknowledge my father to make the story short. My father, also, is not very particular on acknowledgment. In fact, he hates it.

So yes, I let it go and decided to pursue another topic which would seem safer and in line to what I do best at that time. Swimming. I needed to graduate. I needed to earn my degree. I needed to become an Architect. That was what matters at that time. In the pursuit of my coveted profession, I sacrificed a topic that I love so I can get what I've always aspired to be: *An Architect*.

As earlier discussed, I found out it wasn't enough for me. I needed more from life. So, I left for New York City. I was going to study International Affairs but the program at a University near Union Square was more about *political science*. I wasn't even aware that my graduate program was leading me back to my long-lost bachelor's thesis topic: The ORP.

I thought that since I'm spending my own money for a master's degree that I don't really need to help me in my practical life, I might as well pursue a thesis topic that I've always been yearning to write about. I literally had to start from scratch because my writing style has significantly changed. It means, my writing has somewhat matured.

Although, my master's thesis advisor would refer to my use of words as archaic still. When I presented the idea to my thesis writing professor; as usual, I was met with significant number of criticisms. I was prepared for it. I was stubborn. I was thinking that since this is my money, why can't I write a thesis that I really want? I want to enjoy this process. This was the only reward I could give to myself after three years of being in a program that I couldn't quite understand what I'm in for. In order for me to get a better job, I have to enroll to a PhD program or enroll in a business school. I wasn't sure I was going to pursue either so while not being sure, I thought, I might as well enjoy this final chapter of my master's program. And I gave it my all because I had no intention of coming back. I just wanted it over but I needed to be motivated to finish the program. The ORP was my motivation.

I worked on the ORP for six months a semester before and took my *Research Methods* class at the Graduate Faculty. My professor, a clinical psychologist, gave me an A. He was a very generous man but I don't think he was stupid or that he was giving me an A, just because. I believe it was a well-deserved A.

The following semester, I enrolled for the thesis track. The thesis track was not graded. It's only a pass/fail requirement. For completion purposes. This means, that it's only sole purpose of being is for the student to give one final product after all the course program has been completed. I completed all 42 credits with a 3.7 GPA. Anyone who understands the GPA system would know that I wasn't one of those graduate students struggling *academically*.

I used to recall getting so attached with an A. When I found out from one of my first year first semester class that I can actually re-write my paper to get a better grade, I was ecstatic! Never have I heard of such privilege in the Philippines. I understood that the professors were appreciative of the effort as opposed to just settling for a passing grade. I thought that this culture was consistent all across the graduate program. But when I had Abdoumalique Simone finally as my professor (1st semester of my 2nd year) and I did the same in his class (although he was very patient and generous), I also began to realize that I was demanding more from him than I should. In not so many words, I was realizing that I was no longer focusing on the learning but on my grades. I realized, that wasn't what I was in graduate studies for to begin with. I was in the program because of him – because of what he described I will learn. Since his class, I stopped caring what I get for my grades and focused on *learning* as much as I can.

So, I chose my 1st and 2nd Readers. The 1st one was a previous professor who also gave me an A. His name was David Gold. The 2nd reader was also a previous professor, who gave me a well-deserved B+ in her previous class. Let's call her Professor K. Both of these professors knew my academic performance. Both of them have graded my paper. Both of them knew my academic integrity and not once was my integrity ever been questioned.

From within the department, I had another professor from Argentina. She was a sweet professor. I thought she was nice. She was the first professor that told me that my writing does not have citations. She believed I wasn't being dishonest but I needed to provide citations on my final paper. She gave me an A still. She even said that what I have submitted was beyond what she asked and that I gave more than was asked of me. I was extremely thankful to her for that gesture and since that time, I made the effort to always visit the university writing center. It would seem unfortunate that academic writing in the Philippines or at least in my university was not yet as evolved as that in the US. I realized I was lagging behind. But since then, I had been a constant visitor of the university writing center. My relationship with this professor didn't end here though. It led into something so politically charged that left a very bad taste leading to a hostile environment for me within the department.

Since my 1st Reader was always busy, I ended up consulting my 2nd Reader more often. She knew she was just my 2nd Reader. She later asked me to inform my 1st Reader that she will be my 1st Reader since she was the one spending more time with me, of which Mr. Gold agreed.

I was working closely with Professor K for six months while during the week, I fly across the country doing my consulting work. I had a full-time job already. During the wee hours of the morning before I go to work, I would write my thesis. I would sleep for an hour or so then leave for work. One can only imagine how I managed to survive such ordeal.

It is important to note that for the most part of this consultation, she had supported and *approved* my working drafts, which lead me to believe that I was heading on the right direction. Just two weeks prior to my graduation, I finally submitted my final draft installment to Professor K; when all of a sudden, she yells at me and tells me that my thesis was not good enough. She told me I was not fit to graduate. She told me my English was archaic. I remembered her telling me very clearly that I am better off returning to the Philippines where I belong. She told me I should start from scratch. For someone, who had been working very diligently, this interaction was quite a shocker and humiliating. For someone who had been working more than 40 hours a week, it would seem very difficult to take comments like that lightly. I broke down. Since I broke down, she realized at that moment what she had done. She told me to revise my thesis, hire an editor over the weekend and submit it to her as soon as possible. However, because I was emotionally distressed and needed to speak with someone, I went to the university Graduate Faculty hoping to speak with just anyone. I did not intend to speak with the Associate Dean but that's where I ended up anyways. Since I was emotionally distressed, the Associate Dean had advised me to go to the counselor. And so, I did and told the counselor everything.

The Associate Dean obviously contacted Professor K. Professor K retaliated and sent me an email informing me that she was rejecting my thesis because it wasn't good enough and she realized that she didn't have enough grounds to reject my thesis or at least get rid of me. She accused me of plagiarism on a thesis draft that was still a work-in-progress in order to formally get rid of me.

My ultimate crime then was that I failed to perfectly and completely provide *in-text* citations in some of my paragraphs. I was dismissed from my program after three years of hard work by an academic committee panel that consisted of the same advisor who accused me and un-tenured administrative staff handpicked by the Associate Dean. I had the misfortune of choosing a "so-called" celebrity professor whose known credibility was only because she was the granddaughter of the former prime minister of the former multinational conglomeration. She later wrote a book advocating the value of individual freedom. I used to remember gritting my teeth wondering how one can fake a work of such hypocrisy.

Plagiarism is such a convenient tool for many academic professors to sabotage anyone that is not within their liking or for those that challenges their thinking. Unfortunately, or fortunately (depending on where one is coming from) for private educational institutions, they are protected by the US legal system. It is so easy to catch any one of plagiarism. I am quite certain that if the whole school will be purposefully round up, all students including professors, would be guilty of *technical* plagiarism. Academic writing is not easy – even seasoned writers such as Martin Luther King Jr. or famous historian, Doris Kearns Goodwin faced charges of plagiarism. I recall Professor K telling me that I was not liked by many people in the department. I used to recall asking how that information had anything to do with my thesis and asked her if what she's doing (engaging in departmental gossip) was proper or ethical since she was my thesis adviser after all. She justified her behavior as part of her professional privileges. I was quite disappointed then to realize that no degree of education can guarantee values and a sense of justice.

I'm not referring to any formal education but higher education in particular wherein we come in primarily as adults with the willingness to learn more and beyond what we already know to be better professionals and/or people. One would hope that achieving such endeavor would entail learning about effective communications& cultivating personal discipline to be respectful of others. I observed that generally, most people show respect and care only in situations applicable in formal and business settings. One tends to forget what one learns when dealing with people in informal settings where one is not visible by an audience that does not directly matter professionally. I guess self-righteousness is one pitfall that comes with educational attainment. One's *Curriculum Vitae* indicating a person's educational attainment is not the real judge of a person's character and abilities of how can one sustainably succeed in any endeavor.

Admittedly, I am aware that I wasn't very much liked by a few professors primarily because I was quite aggressive with my arguments. I grew up having to constantly fight for my ideas especially against my father. My professors often found my ideas too provocative and ambitious. I noticed that almost everyone in my university hated the United States of America. They hated being an American. The professors hated everything about the United States. Since I am a Filipino, I am naturally an American lover. I grew up watching Hollywood movies. I loved everything American and that's why I was enrolled in a US University because I loved America. It was just to my surprise that the US was the most hated country in that university smack in the middle of New York City.

I noticed that our program director and his wife were hoping I would learn to hate the US as much as they did. They didn't tell me this of course but I later realize the source of their antagonism towards me. I caught him and his wife purposefully manipulating my grades. How did I do that? It was a three-panel class that included him, his wife and another professor. The wife was my Argentinian professor. Throughout the duration of the semester, neither of them would take the time to schedule a meeting with me to discuss different topics for my final paper. I participated well in class and always submitted my papers on time. When I received my grade for my final paper, I thought it was kind of odd that my final grade was the same as my paper grade. She also attached a page long summary statement about my personality. The feedback was not very academic – I felt like

I was a 10-year-old kid receiving a detention letter from my teacher to be given to my parents. I was paranoid but I also knew with certainty that something wasn't right. I tried to schedule a meeting with either of the three but none of them would meet with me in person. So, I went to the office of our program director without an appointment and luckily, he was available or at least he wasn't able to come up with an excuse. I asked him how I could further improve my paper so that I would not repeat the same mistakes in the future. I asked him to go over my paper with me and as he was reading along with me, it was obvious that he never read my paper. So luckily, he wasn't able to prepare his grade-breaking criticisms to support his stance. He understood my paper and he couldn't pretend that he didn't in front of me. He later made excuses that I add transition phrases between paragraphs, delete a few sentences, and later changed my grade from B- to A-. I didn't really care much about my grade anymore. The last thing on my mind was my grade since I was more focused on the *hunch*. I just felt the need to know if they were indeed manipulating my grades. Before I left his office, he told me I should be careful since I still have one more year to go with the program. I thanked him for that and didn't notice the veiled threat. I got my confirmation that I was not being treated fairly and that was enough for me. I thought I was safe since I figured out a way to avoid them. I took classes outside of the department so none of them could manipulate my grades anymore. None of them ever attempted to fail me though. I always thought no one could fail me. I've always been confident of my abilities especially in writing. But my self-confidence had been put to the ultimate test when I got accused of plagiarism. I realized; I couldn't defend myself because I was indeed guilty of "technical plagiarism" but I wasn't guilty of dishonesty. However, nobody cared whether I was dishonest or not. All my professors wanted were to get me out of the program – to remove all my associations with their program because I didn't fit in their profile of graduates even if I had a 3.7 GPA. Obviously, I am a very loyal person and I don't change stripes so easily. When they realized this after two years of trying to change the way I think, they decided to take some drastic measures since I was the only odd one left in the program that didn't subscribe to their ideology. I was the only republican in the entire university, probably. At that time, I didn't know I was a republican. I always thought I was a democrat. I loved Hillary Clinton. I admired Bill Clinton. But that wasn't enough to make me a democrat. I only realized later that I have more in common with republicans than I do democrats.

I found it disconcerting at that time that certain educators were given the absolute power to destroy a student's academic career. I am generalizing of course but it would be safe to say that having experienced a first-hand injustice of academics at an overpriced university near Union Square, I guess, my statement carried some truth to it. Given that I was indeed high strung and arrogant, does it justify this form of abuse? At worst, I may deserve a failing grade or in this particular case she could just merely rejected my thesis or gave me an incomplete as what she originally threatened.

I later surmised why I am not surprised why there was so much injustice in this world because even in a civilized environment, injustice prevailed and still prevail. I would think that injustice lurks strongest in places where no one suspects – be it in a church or in an educational institution. Politics – a word that carried so much pain and misery yet considered as an accepted norm in society. – *From this statement alone, I was already angry with the church as of this time.*

It is easy to find a lawyer that will defend institutions and professors, but very rarely (or even non-existent) to find a lawyer that will fight for students unless it had something to do with sexual harassment. Still, I was lucky. I had a lawyer – a corporate one, who didn't normally handle small cases like mine but took pity on me and took on my case. Although it wasn't his area of specialization, he did gave it his best shot and his argument wasn't weak. Except that we used a weak strategy by suing the university instead of suing my professor. The university also hired one of the best law firms in the state, that specialized on cases like mine. In fairness, my lawyer was really good. He was sincere and eloquent. He was a very charismatic man and I honestly felt comforted that he took on my case even if his fee was so little. I paid a little over $20,000 for a case that lasted for almost three years. It was a bargain. If any, his role in my life then was similar to that of a counselor. He knew how to pacify me when I would get paranoid and angry. He was very patient up to the very end. Although we lost the case both on the lower court and the appeal, I still felt that I have won. The case dragged on for about two years and it gave me enough time to pick up myself. It bought me time – time to hope, time to dream, and time to heal.

I hope for anyone out there seeking for a sense of justice, belonging, and meaning in an environment where one is rendered helpless that they find comfort that there is a way out. There's no crime in fighting back. I may have lost a lot of money but I gained my dignity back and that made all my struggle worthwhile.

I hope to have painted an authentic and clearer picture of various illusions of success, failure, joy and sadness of an ordinary person's struggle to find oneself in New York City. I do not have the credibility that comes in association with a reputable academic institution – but I only have a story to tell. I always felt the need to verbalize and concretize all the painful events that happened in my life so I can finally accept and learn to live with them. I couldn't find enough time to go to a shrink then due to my full-time job. Even if I could, I still wouldn't. It just isn't the lifestyle I grew up with. The best that I could do was simply to write about it. Writing, indeed, is the best form of therapy.

But where Am I now with this part of my life?

I wrote all of the above at the time when I was still so broken. I kept all the narrative to demonstrate that at the time I wrote this, I was still in a state of trauma. I was trying to justify my actions. The truth was, I realized after so many years, and after going thru years of *purification* where I have learned how to understand God's language, that all of the above happened because God was saving me from a fate worse than death. If I continued to stay in New York City then - if I wasn't expelled, I would have grown my pride further.

While I was living in International House, New York, which I will discuss further in the next chapter, I was elected by over 500 residents coming from over 100 countries across the globe to be part of the Resident Council. It was the first real election that I ever won in my life, and it had to be in the international arena. I had the second greatest number of votes so I was able to select the position

I wanted. I selected being a *Resident Trustee for Programs and Life* because it allowed me to have a seat at the table with fellow International House trustees. To name a few, *David Rockefeller*, *Paul Volcker*, the *Dodge* couple, *Fareed Zakariah*, the *Soros* couple (brother or cousin of George Soros) and so many more. I was very ambitious. I had a great plan in mind for my career. I wanted to be in the field of Foreign Affairs, as an ambassador. I have met the most powerful people in the world in one lunch table. Literally. I had complete awareness that those people seated in that table have the power to choose the leaders in any country in the whole world, and buy out any business in any country if they wanted to. They were literally the most powerful and richest of the super-rich. I often wondered what was God's reason for allowing me to meet them? For allowing me to get that far? I thought they would be fearsome like the politicians I used to hear about in my country. Or like the wealthy businessmen that my father dealt with. But they were not fearsome at all. They were human. And kind. And that was the last of their leadership. For many years, they had controlled the world. Following that, was a world less controlled, with different unknown powers coming from whichever. Chaos was no longer controlled. Nothing seemed controlled. But what was the point here? None of those people had the power not to die or to not let people die. None. So, *power* and *wealth*, simply cannot stop death from happening and that these people we fear? were mere human beings – just like us.

If I had succeeded in my life in the direction that I hoped, I could very well reach great heights. I was already in the presence of very powerful people who can make or break anyone. If I had succeeded transforming myself with distorted values, I would have lost myself completely to a life separated from the Lord. I used to ask God, "why did you let me go so far, let me smell success, let me taste greatness, and just take it all away in one fell swoop?" and God answered "I let you go as far as your heart desired because you were begging me for it but if I didn't stop you, I would have lost you completely."

It took me over 20 years to heal from what happened to me, only to realize, I only have gratitude in my heart because they were instrumental in saving my soul. When we look at things from human eyes, it would seem, life is cruel. If we look at adversity from human eyes, we would rest on the anguish. But if we look at things from God's eyes, we start to appreciate all the efforts God had to do to save us from ourselves; from our choices; from our desires that will feed into our vanity – and vanity is *Pride*. Pride the highest form of evil. In 2017, God let me experience his supernatural power – the power to bring me back to life. God let me experienced the true power of allowing me to witness the full extent of my mortality, which I will discuss in another chapter in full detail.

I am deeply aware of the criticisms of people when I speak of my spiritual journey. I still have many influential people in my network. But why am I unashamed to speak about God? Because of the certainty that there cannot be anyone in this universe, spiritual or incarnate, more powerful than God. I eventually understood why God allowed me to meet those many powerful people so that when I get to this point in my life where I get to glorify God's name, and I feel a sense of trepidation of the profile of my audience, God can always remind me and say, "remember the most powerful people I allowed you to meet? No one can ever be more powerful than those people and most of them are gone." No one person can ever be in control of anyone. No one. Only God. People's disbelief or lack of knowledge of God will not stop their misery, their tragedy, and their demise. Therefore, I choose to speak of the Lord because he is the only true celebrity the world needs to know of and no other.

I never thought I would reach a point now that when I think of my professor, I would feel a sense of gratitude. While I now vaguely recall how she seemed evil in my eyes back then? wherein I would even get nightmares and I would scream in the middle of the night in great fury, I can finally think of her now with compassion for all the hate that I used to feel for her. While those people whom I thought worked in cohorts with her would seem as evil as I wrote it above? but they actually weren't. They were doing their job exactly how God permitted them to do to stop me. I needed to be put on my knees, once and for all. My pride was going out of control. If that didn't happen, I could have destroyed many lives. I needed to be humbled. God did everything to bring me home. That was actually the words my professor told me, "Go back to the Philippines, where you belong". Back then, I felt so offended because I thought she was discriminating me. But now? I couldn't be more thankful that I am back in the Philippines. This is indeed where I belong. The spiritual protection I got in Cebu is truly what had been protecting me all my life the entire time I was growing up. It's no wonder why my father got so angry when I decided to leave for New York City, which I will explain in full detail in the next chapter too.

RECOGNIZING VICTORY

I come from Cebu, the island in the heart of the Philippines – an archipelago of 7,107 islands. It's a country equipped with one of the most bountiful natural resources in the world. But I did not come from a place of luxury. In fact, I remember my family was struggling for the most part of my childhood. It wasn't until I was in high school that our financial situation significantly changed towards the better. I didn't have a lot of friends as I was growing up. I used to play with homeless children in the streets or those living in the most extreme impoverished conditions. Back then, the awareness that those kids were poor never seemed to have crossed my mind. My siblings were way older than me then so I was never invited to play with them. I don't blame them – I was too small and I was my father's favorite. In a way, they didn't want to take any responsibility just in case something happened to me.

When I was in first grade – I got a star. I was awarded the best in math. I was not even aware I was good in math. I didn't even think I was trying at all. However, this was the time when recognition came with a huge price. Some people just don't know how to handle it and I was one of those. Since I've never been recognized for anything until that day, I grabbed on to it. With recognition, I immediately came up with an "illusion" of power. At such a young age, I felt the pressure of holding on to something and getting so attached by what it represents. **Recognition**. What a big daunting word. I was so full of pride and could not handle the possibility of not getting a star the next time around. I was afraid of disappointing my teacher so I cheated on my Roman Numerals. It was an easy subject – very easy yet I sacrificed my self-respect and cheated merely because I wanted to be sure I will get a good grade without realizing what I was losing in the process. My teacher, of course, caught me and the disappointment in her face erased all the recognition I felt when she gave me a star. I was so ashamed. I don't know what happened to that star but I clearly remember it losing its value because of what I did. Cheating is bad – no matter what. This was my first big lesson in life. I learned it at grade one.

One day during the summer prior to starting 2nd grade, I turned into a corner and my brother's friend hit me in the eye with a tin cap they used as bullets on a wooden gun they made themselves. I was blinded – not permanently, but for a couple of months. I lost my eyesight on my left eye for quite some time. I had been lucky because I got my eyesight back; although, my left eye was red while I went to school. I looked kind of hideous then. I am born with a pink mark on my face. Not a small mark, but almost like a map of my province on my left cheek. I've always been ridiculed (or bullied, whichever sound graver) because of my birth mark but I have learned to fight at an early age because of that. After my eye accident, I had to deal with my birthmark on my face and a red eye that remained red for almost a year; my hair was short and frizzy. I was a skinny little girl and was badly dressed. My skirts were up to my knees – uneven. My white shirt was dirty – since I didn't really know how to be neat back then. My mom was very busy taking care of business because my dad was in Manila working. I was left in the care of the help, who also had too much work at home. We were each left to take care of ourselves. My classmates would call me names – children can be so mean sometimes. Of course, they didn't really know what they were doing so I can't blame them.

I never thought of myself as a beautiful girl but probably as a defense mechanism, I was always oozing with confidence, so they say. My advantage was that, I've always had that innate leadership and entrepreneurial skills that kept me occupied while I was growing up. Somehow, all the meanness was cushioned a bit and didn't prevent me from developing my self-confidence more- sometimes to a point of arrogance.

I always managed to win friends despite my sour disposition even without trying. I had that "Despicable Me" persona. I have been an angry kid. A lot of children did not like me, but somehow, amidst all those angry kids – a friend always stood by me. There were quite a handful of them each year. I didn't develop a relationship with them but they seemed to develop one with me (without me being aware of it since I don't remember their names and faces). Regardless, I do remember having them around. I never really got to appreciate their role in my life back in those days. I wouldn't say I took advantage of them or took them for granted because I was barely aware they were there for me until much later in life…like much later.

I learned the true value of integrity when I joined my high school varsity swimming team. I learned that victory is not about winning or losing but on how the game is played. I learned that the true essence of sportsmanship is in the conquering of the self and putting up a good fight. I always remember the many wisdoms my swimming coach from my high school varsity days, Coach Lando, often imparted to motivate us and it is to know that one has done one's very best in everything one aimed to do. I always believed that there is no failure when one has done one's very best. Recognition is only icing on the cake- it doesn't stick but the learning experience does. It took me a while to own my victories, and learned to avoid getting swayed by noises that kept on preventing me from claiming those victories.

I always loved writing. When I was little, I found an electronic typewriter at my dad's office. Little would be around 10 years old. I noticed that so many things happened when I was just 10 years old. It was the age where I discovered the late Ferdinand Marcos was my hero. It was the age that I became socially and academically active in school. It was the age where I revealed that I wasn't just a wall flower and it was the age where I was driven to win oratorical and declamation contests.

10 was my age of enlightenment. I remember, I would watch a movie and if I don't like the ending, I'd end up writing an entirely new story, with an entirely different ending. The movie I used to watch were romantic dramas -some right from a TV series.

After school, I find myself rapidly typing on that electronic keyboard since we didn't have a computer yet at that time.

I wrote a lot. I remember my brother's girlfriend having read it and she told me how *gifted* I was, and sometimes, I wondered if my writing influenced her life choices since she seemed to have emulated one of my characters in one of my stories. I get that kind of compliment from my brothers' friends and girlfriends all the time but I never really get why. I kept receiving gifts from them telling me how *gifted* I was. Seriously. All I cared about then was, I really wanted to write. I needed to write. I just have to. Even then, I didn't keep any of the stories I wrote. Somehow, everything I wrote just disappear and I never really thought of keeping them. I just write and write and write without really thinking for who and why. I just knew, I have a story in my head and I just need to write it out.

In high school, I organized a princess club. I was princess of the universe. And what princesses in my club did was to write full page novels. I tend to set the rules pretty often when I was young. At this time, I had to write by hand since I couldn't bring the heavy electronic typewriter to school. The idea then was to fill a half inch notebook with a novel. This was the time when I learned to read romantic novels. Man, it was hard. I remember having a hard time coming up with an ending. Writing novels was just way too long for my taste especially that it was hand-written.

Then came the computer. I remember the first time I learned to use the computer. I don't recall how I got one but I recall my friend, Cathy, teaching me how to use it and the internet. I remember being so blown away. It was the beginning of the end. I was so hooked. I spend every waking minute of every day on the internet. It used to be only mIRC (Internet Relay Chat Client).

When I was in college, I got involved in a bitch fight. Typical fighting with girls over a guy thing that I originally met online. The situation then was pretty desperate and it was either I explain why I got involved in a bitch fight or suffer suspension or expulsion for it. This happened two years after Simone died. I opened myself up to a guy through the internet, whom I eventually met in person, and was the ex-boyfriend of someone that also went to my university. That girl belonged to a group, we call in the Philippines, as "barkada". I never really belong in that kind of friendship, perhaps briefly after college, as I am mostly into a one-on-one kind of friendship. After meeting my cyber chat mate, I became extremely paranoid. I always had trust issues so I started suspecting he was with other women. Although the label we gave each other were best friends, but we were actually not being "friendly" with each other. It was a mutual adult relationship without any proper label. I felt jealous and insecure. It didn't help me that his ex-girlfriend and her group was making fun of me. This scenario was my very first experience of adult bullying. One afternoon, I knew that these girls would be in the cafeteria or we would call it *canteen*. I asked a male classmate if he could accompany me since I suspected that I might get bullied. But he refused. I had foresight at what could happen but because of my pride, I didn't want to feel afraid. So, I went to the canteen and I was bullied as I had foreseen it. A girl grabbed my hair from behind me and my instincts just took over. The ex-girlfriend reported me to the school security.

That was my first litigation case. I was my own lawyer and I pretty much wrote everything from memory; including the conversations, the interpretation, even the smallest of details. It was the first case that I won. I was, of course, reprimanded but the other was expelled. The expulsion was not entirely my doing but because the other already had plenty of academic cases filed against her. My case was just the final straw.

I later confessed this to a priest who reprimanded me that I committed sin the moment I decided to go to the canteen. He said I should have avoided the conflict granting that I already had prior foresight of what was going to happen. I believed I was remorseful then. I understood it. Since then, I avoided going out until the situation calmed down. And the situation eventually died down.

I proceeded to writing poems. I got me an internet boyfriend all the way to Florida who happened to enjoy writing poems too. Although, it was interesting that the only reason we got connected was because I accused him of hacking my ICQ. It's actually the original Text lingo, short for "I SEEK YOU". I even recall speaking the language of hacking and using crack codes and keygens to access certain programs to get access to free internet. Since not many people back then knew how to troubleshoot a PC interface, we sometimes use coding within the DOS or Linux interface. I used to be language savvy with coding lingo back in the days. From writing TV series scripts, to novels, to affidavits, to poetry, to coding and hacking, and so many more. I must say my internet savviness really helped me with my architecture classes. At that time, I was one or may have been the only female in my class that produced full set thesis floor plans using AutoCAD (computer aided design) software at that time. That skill was very useful when I went to New York and helped me find day jobs as an auto cad drafter to keep ends meet. That guy who got me into the bitch-fight was a whiz with it so I got advanced drafting lessons from him compared to my local counterparts. He was also the one who introduced me to hardcore porn. Literally full-blown tutorials. This I will discuss later.

It was also through the internet that I learned how to develop romantic relationships with the opposite sex. Although I was in the varsity all throughout my high school years and most of my companions were male but I've always been one of the guys. I would have suitors and crushes but sadly, I never felt any real connection. However, I did over the internet not once but countless times. Why? Because the medium of communication was in writing. But I also did so because of my commitment to my college best friend, Simone (who tragically passed away more than a year before), that I will give people a chance. I had a very strong awareness already that I am not emotionally healthy. I even told my internet or cyber best friend (sort of boyfriend) that I never really expected to have a healthy relationship.

I think my reading comprehension worked better than verbal back then. I think and respond faster when I'm reading and writing as oppose to listening and talking. I think it must be because I have a self-diagnosed *attention deficit hyperactivity disorder* (*ADHD*)? I would have to say that the internet did have much to do with my socializing skills, which came very useful when I moved to New York City. I met so many amazing people even in the Philippines that otherwise would have deemed impossible since we belong in different social circles. At the time, only very few people had access to the internet, let alone owned a computer. I recall billing my dad over 40,000 pesos a month for internet usage and that was only the 90's. My dad, of course, condoned it because it kept me at home all the time. I guess it was better than keeping track of me. It made real life interaction with people a breeze and everything just came so naturally.

I've heard that getting your first million is the hardest thing to do but once you get it, the next million will be easy. What I didn't realize then was that they were referring to a different currency – the US dollar. I earned my first million in Philippine Currency when I was 24 years old (although a classmate of mine earned his at age 16 – he was in the real estate business then. I heard he did so just for the fun of it). To count my blessings, I was able to single-handedly close five multi-million projects from new clients – clients my father never heard of before. I got them because of my circle of friends that my parents barely knew about and my inherent salesmanship skills. I was and still am socially active. My family was very conservative and pragmatic. They used to disapprove of my social life as they think it was a waste of money even if I wasn't really spending much. My friends were pretty smart when it came to partying- they always get in for free; consequently, so did I.

I've always been thinking of a good investment that did not entail a lot of capital. My father has always been tough when it came to business. He was never the type who spoon-fed us. It's what he called, **tough love**. He said that if I want to start my own business, I should do so using my own money and I should start low- meaning zero capital from him. True enough, I tried to start an exporting business by selling knitted bikinis. I had a friend who manufactured export-quality bikinis and I was getting it at a wholesale price. The bikinis were selling well within the Philippines and the return of investment was pretty good but not large enough. My earnings were pennies compared to how much I was earning developing business and finding clients for my dad's company. Regardless, I wanted more and something that I can call mine to begin with. In the spring of 2004, I decided to take a three-month vacation in the US to look for potential buyers for my knitted bikinis. I brought approximately 100 pairs of bikinis with me but realized I had no clue how to sell them to boutiques or retail stores since I never really had enough experience in the fashion retail industry. I ended up selling my bikinis to my sister's friends, which sold pretty well but still not large enough to be sustainable.

As I was tossing around my sister's bed at 3 am in the morning, I was feeling hopelessly frustrated with my business endeavor since I really wanted it to work. I was impatient. I always had the habit of learning how to run first before walking and over the years, it worked for me. I wanted to have a business that could go international. I thought I'd apply to a fashion school but when I went there, I was turned off by their projection of my potential salary after graduation. It was ridiculously low and it would have taken me forever before I could pay off my loans. My sister who was working as a medical technologist in Long Island, New York was insisting that I should take up nursing instead. That was actually the reason why I was bringing my transcript with me. So, one day, I decided to visit my former college friend in the city. I stayed in her midget-sized room and she was kind enough to share her bunk bed with me. During the day, she would go to class and I would walk around Union Square. My friend was also kind enough to give me access to the University's computer lab.

While I was surfing the web, I was surfing for potential courses I might possibly be interested in even though I had no idea if I could afford an education in the US. Suddenly, I saw an ad, *"Orientation for the Graduate Program in International Affairs – today at 6 PM"*. I thought, I'd just check it out. I went and attended the orientation. AbdouMaliq Simone, an urbanist and sociologist, was leading the orientation. It was because of him that I decided to enroll in that program. I was able to bring him to Cebu in 2011, as a keynote speaker for **The Movement for a Livable Cebu (MLC),** a non-profit I co-founded to stop the construction of fly-overs in Cebu city, just months before we founded an international film festival, which I will briefly mention later. I initially just wanted to help my former college professor back in architecture school, whom I was courting to be one of the board members of the film festival I founded by suggesting a more academic approach to protesting. We utilized the collaborative method that I used for my non-profit, Omnilogy, which I also founded before leaving New York city. I will also discuss that later. MLC was much bigger, multi-sectoral and the stakeholders involved were quite influential. It turned out to be very successful because we got a moratorium against the construction of fly-overs from the undersecretary of the Department of Public Works and Highways (DPWH). This moratorium remained valid even to date. AbdouMaliq was very instrumental in getting us this victory.

Going back to him during the orientation, he said that the course would study as to why there were people living with less than $1/day, find solutions to various social problems, and compare how the market changes across the globe and what globalization was all about. Yes, globalization – the word I've been following over time. The program just sounded like music to my ears. I was so hungry to learn things that would inspire me and, on that day, he did inspire me. He became my professor later on. I think he was one of the most brilliant professors I've ever had in my life. He was not the conventional type of professor. I never had a dull moment in his class. Most professors would teach you how to think outside of the box but he would teach us how to think from inside the box and getting out of it. He would dissect every possible detail that could affect the big picture from a limited position. I didn't think I was one of his favorites but I knew I could trust him. There were only two professors I trusted in my program but both of them stopped teaching at my department before I could complete my program. Perhaps, if he were still in the program, I would have been spared from the injustice and abuse I later experienced from certain faculty members. I don't think he would have tolerated injustice under his watch. He was known for being fair and there was a point that I thought he fought for me even if he didn't like me – that was my assumption of course. He was truly a professional in every aspect.

I immediately applied for the program. I easily got accepted in the program. My friend did try to discourage me and said I should check out Columbia University before I decide. I did check it out – online. Their requirements were pretty steep and the waiting period seemed longer -like an entire semester. I couldn't wait to live in New York anymore. At that moment, I just needed to be in New York City more than I wanted to breathe. I came home in the Philippines informing my dad of my decision.

Contrary to what most parents feel when they find out their daughter got accepted to a US University, my dad was heartbroken and so was my mom (mostly because of the fear of the expense). I never had a history of doing anything that opposed my parents' will until then. My dad was so angry he threatened that he wouldn't give me a penny to support me. My parents never approved of my coming to New York to begin with. My dad insisted it's unnecessary since we have a family business that needed me. Problem was, I didn't want to work for the family business. Although I do care a lot for our people; it just wasn't the life I imagined living at that time. I just didn't feel accomplished. I wanted to start something that was really mine from the very beginning. Working for the family did not allow me to do that because there were so many variables to consider. One of those variables was my father. My dad is a generous man but he is tough with us – his children. Despite his tough love, I still lived a sheltered life. Of course, I wasn't unaware of the evils of the world, but I've always thought I could handle them.

When I first stepped in the halls of my Graduate Program in International Affairs in the fall of 2004, I knew something was very wrong. Everything was just not going right. I had problems with my medical records and the entire registration process was just a mess. I've always had an instinct of what is not good for me. I was depressed and I finally admitted that I made a very huge mistake. I went to the Assistant Director and told him of my decision. I told him, *"I could have spent my money on a similar program in the Philippines and I would still get my degree. Before it's too late, I would like to withdraw so I can get my money back."* Although he agreed that I will still get a similar degree but he highlighted that it would not be a US degree, and that makes a lot of difference. He then said, *"Before you decide, why don't you think about it overnight because you may just be feeling homesick".* A part of me knew that something was wrong, but I decided to give myself more time to consider it. I went home feeling very depressed. Elizabeth, my roommate was home, and I told her of my decision. On a side note, the apartment I was living in was a three-bedroom townhouse and their old roommate just left them – I became the new roommate. The apartment was very beautiful and cheap, and located in Brooklyn. However, she didn't have a full-time job and my other roommate (my friend who I used to bunk in with while she was still living in the University dorm) still lived on minimum wage at that time. Anyways, Elizabeth was amazing. She was not known for her patience during the little time that I've known of her, but she had the patience to talk to me that night and succeeded in talking me out of my leaving New York. What really talked me out was my pride. I wanted to prove to my parents that I could be sustainable – that I can live on my own and survive it. I was ashamed to fly back home in just two weeks and admit defeat. At that time, I thanked God, then for my pride. Little did I know that this decision would lead me to my rock bottom moment. A nagging fear I've been trying to outwit my way out of.

I've always loved to seek adventure – to take risks and seek out further possibilities. When I finished college and got my license as a professional Architect– I started to feel the reality of being a grown up and the responsibilities that came with it. I started feeling afraid. I didn't like feeling afraid. I don't like to fear life. I don't like to fear anything. I felt that there was something out there that I haven't seen nor experienced yet. I just needed to get out there. I needed to know what it was like out there. I thought, if I end up returning home, at least I've known of it. And so, I surely did. Big time.

MY FIRST MILLION –
A NEW YORK LIFE

New York City

How can such city be so marvelous?
Each day in this magnificent place,
Is like falling in love

If New York is a guy,
I will be his slave,
This place has captivated me
--- Like how a lover would…

New York! New York!
I have fallen for you…
If poetry can take shape
I'll shape it like New York.

In this city, I have learned of real pain,
The agony of falling…
Yet it is in this city

That I have truly healed...
The scar is invisible –
The pain has transformed...
A feeling akin to passion ---
Oh yes, I am alive again!

I t wasn't so long ago when I felt that I was on top of the world – or that's what I thought it was. There was a moment that I felt loved by everyone – everyone being everyone I cared about or thought I cared about. I lived in an environment where people outside of it would think it is a myth. I lived in *International House, New York* – or I-House, for brevity. A lot of former residents tried to write literary pieces about their experiences but it is quite difficult to write about <u>International House</u>.

International House is like a whole country that consists of residents coming from over 100 countries around the world. It consisted of talented and well-rounded individuals who came to New York to pursue their graduate or post-graduate studies or were doing their internships. It is a place where one can have lunch with someone so humble but brilliant like *David Rockefeller*, get scolded by someone so dynamic like *Colin Powell* (I interrupted him so I can get his autograph of his autobiographical book while he was conversing with someone), but get comforted or motivated while on the same table by someone so accomplished like *John C. Whitehead*, or attend a board meeting in the presence of someone so huge, both literal and philosophical, like the former Federal Reserve Chairman, *Paul Volcker*, and last but not the least, to sit in conversation with someone so amazingly witty and charismatic like the diplomat and 2008 Nobel Prize Awardee, *Marrti Ahtisaari*. The experiences that

one can get in that community can be so overwhelming –
it is so difficult to know where to start, which stories to
choose and how to end it. The end used to be very difficult
for me to picture because with it also carried hope and
disillusionment.

That feeling of being loved borders illusion and reality – for
it was just my feeling – unconfirmed illusions. The feeling
was real though. I was living in I-House and I've never felt
more alive. It was the one time I can remember that I was
truly happy – but that illusion of happiness didn't last long.
That illusion of happiness wasn't straightforward either – it
was like a flash of light that comes and goes and sometimes,
it was stable enough that the light doesn't dim for a while.
Then that was it.

Every once and a while, that flash of happiness would find
me, but in terms of seconds within the span of light years.
I wondered how many people like me experience this kind
of elusive joy? I did feel it though – I'm sure I did because
I wouldn't have missed it so much causing me pain upon
recollection if they didn't happen.

I've had so many good and painful memories in the past
but I don't recall missing them as much as the first two
years I've lived in New York City. I lived in New York for
almost four years and the remaining time following the
first two great years was the beginning of my inevitable
downfall. I've hit rock bottom. I've always heard that at
some point in one's life, one will experience that ultimate
downfall. I always feared it and tried to make every painful
event in my life as large as it can ever be to prevent me
from experiencing a *rock bottom* moment. Oh, how wrong

I was for no amount of psychic warning could prevent any form of human suffering. During this time, I still didn't truly have a clear understanding of what it truly meant to be a Christian. I think I may have a few previous episodes of major downfall but I've always recovered so I guess those episodes weren't real enough except for one – the death of my college best friend, Simone. She drowned during a family reunion. Their boat capsized. She was an unusual saint-like friend; almost a real-life angel. It shook my life in ways I never thought possible. That was my first experience of real grief, a death of someone I didn't know I cared about. It was also the death of my cloistered life. *Grief* – can be a perilous open door and if one is not careful, it becomes a portal for evil to breed.

Prior to my friend's death, I was the most closed, incorrigible, unapproachable, unreachable, arrogant being any friend would avoid. I was unforgiving and famous for holding a grudge. I would cut anyone off before they even begin. My own siblings couldn't stand me as well, because I grew up abused. My parents were always busy so I was left under the care of my two older brothers, who also kept on bickering with each other, and were quite violent too. I recall them throwing frozen fishes at each other straight off the freezer. I would be forced to eat vegetables and if I throw up, my eldest brother would force me to eat what I threw up. I found it difficult to understand because though my age gap with my eldest brother is only seven years, he was treating me like he was an adult that have authority to discipline me with an iron fist. While I saw him to be no close to a child even at such a young age of seven or eight years old, I was already aware of the injustice I felt. It was very disturbing for me because I don't understand why my brother was allowed to beat me that way, while my own father doesn't. Naturally, as a child, I would always tell my father. When my father found out, my father would beat him too. Then my mother would get mad at me because I got my eldest brother into trouble with my father.

To give a proper context why my mother is protective of my eldest brother, and why my father had a short rope with him, who was also physically abused, was because though he was a love-child, he was still conceived outside of marriage, like all of us (actually). This posed a lot of problems not just for the family but also for the child/children.

The **CCC: Part Three: 2353**: explains that Sex outside of marriage is a grave sin and exclude them from sacramental communion.

Now let's check out the **CCC: Part Three: 1640**: "Thus the **marriage bond** has been established by God himself in such a way that a marriage concluded and **consummated** (marital sex) ...between baptized persons can never be dissolved."

Please allow me to translate that in a much simpler way as revealed to me by the grace of the Holy Spirit. The reason why it's absolutely critical for a man and a woman to marry first before having sex is because the sexual act is intended primarily to unite souls (Soul Ties). So, during marriage, thru the "Sacrament of Matrimony" which bonds a couple together, God has sealed and protected their union that it leaves an indelible mark of indissolubility because it is intended to extend one's bloodline. Upon consummation of marriage (marital sex), both souls unite and the Holy Spirit seals their bloodlines together.

Now, what happens if a man and a woman have sex without the *Sacrament of Matrimony*? Souls will unite – bloodlines will unite but without God's seal of protection, it isn't the Holy Spirit that will enter the bloodlines – its preternatural spirits, otherwise called, *demons*. This is how sin enters the bloodline. And this explains why my brother, even though he was an innocent child, was already manifesting an obstinate behavior. The curse caused by fornication outside of marriage was not only limited to my brother alone, but even up to me, and all the way to their children, and their children's children unless they make a sincere effort of cutting the curse. All of us were literally conceived in a state of mortal sin. My parents didn't get God's blessing (marriage in the Roman Catholic Church) until I was 10 years old. And I am the youngest in the family.

As a little boy, my eldest brother was always quite obstinate at a time when both my parents were extremely very poor. My mother was not accepted by my paternal grandmother because she heard that my mother used to be a house helper. What my grandmother didn't know then was that, my mother was made into a house helper by her half-siblings of his father's mistress, whom he lived in cohabitation prior to marrying my maternal grandmother. They separated years after. He went back to his old partner, with the two older half- siblings of my mother conceived outside of marriage. My mother was like Cinderella. She was literally abused by her own half-sister. It is also important to emphasize that my maternal grandfather was 100% pure Chinese from mainland China. His father, which was my maternal great grandfather moved to Camiguin and only had one legitimate son, which was my grandfather, He was the only son he brought with him from China. He was very rich. He pretty much owned most of the land in Camiguin but since he left my grandmother and all his children, he wasn't made aware that my great grandfather assigned his properties all under his name. Even my grandfather didn't know that the land was left under his name. My mother and his siblings only found out about years after when they found one property, and the buyer who have been living in that property bought it from them. So, when my late uncle traced all of the properties in Camiguin, most of the land bore my grandfather's name. When my mom moved to Cagayan, my grandfather forbid her to study because he claimed nobody ever became rich by studying. Since my mom really wanted to finish studying, that's why she decided to be a house helper so that she can get a degree. They were all left to fend for themselves. My paternal grandfather also had a lot of occult practices – burning incense for ancestors and all. He was primarily Buddhist – although my mom was a baptized Catholic. According to my aunt Nelva, who was their second to the youngest, she was only baptized when she was 11 years old. She did recall that my maternal grandmother was very pious and religious. She would go to church everyday and most likely only happened after she separated from my grandfather.

My father was like my mom's knight in shining armor. While my paternal grandmother owned a chain of gasoline stations. My father, who was the eldest, chose to leave with my mother and moved to Manila where she gave birth to my brother. At that time, they barely had anything to eat and my brother according to my aunt, was very naughty and extremely obstinate. My father being desperate and always anxious because he had a wife and a baby, was already at his wits end. He already had suppressed emotions from his own suppressive childhood. My paternal grandfather was quite abusive too. If you notice, the cycle of abuse goes all the way to my paternal great grandfather, and probably way before too. This is how I process our patients in the Ministry of Spiritual liberation by determining, as much as possible, the original source of the contract made with the demonic. I even traced that the mother of my great paternal grandmother was a "Babaylan" – a dancing priestess that dance to the sea and all. This is worship of the demonic. More sin entered our bloodline from her. And also, my maternal grandfather who was Buddhist. I am pretty certain it went all the way back to their own ancestors too. Scripturally (to mean the Roman Catholic Holy Bible), a curse can last up to the fourth (4th) generation (*Exodus 34:7*) and if it remains uncut, will extend to the ninth (9th) to Nineteenth (19th) generation and beyond. This is called a *Generational Curse*.

As far as I know, I am the first one who is consciously making the effort to cut it. How am I cutting it? By offering my own personal sacrifices. By embracing my suffering. A lot of people don't realize the power of one's suffering to heal an entire bloodline. But of course, I'm not saying I have already healed it because it truly depends on the authenticity of my love for God, and only God can determine that. We will only know if my efforts are bearing fruit once my family have transformed and converted like how I have transformed. Let me leave this part for now and continue with my childhood. I will talk more about the concept of sacrifice as a redemptive opportunity God gives to humanity later when I talk about becoming a Catholic again.

My mother was always very frustrated with me because no amount of scolding would get to me. My mother and I were always fighting since I was a little girl. It's not about behavioral differences or similarities but there is actually a demonic source where the conflict was stemming from. It stemmed from the womb. I learned during my paternal grandmother's funeral, where my father's younger brother suddenly called out to me, just plainly out of the blue and said, "you know why you have a red mark on your face"? I was literally surprised why he would even mention it. I have that baffled look on my face. He proceeded in saying, "because your mom tried to abort you". I was already in my early 30's then. I suppressed it of course but the anguish was already building up inside of me. If any, it fortified my pride even further.

My pride, was always a problem for me. The entire time I was growing up, I was constantly bullied and verbally abused and these abuses kept feeding on my pride that I became so angry that I started retaliating. I realized my power and the more I retaliate, I grew harder and more prideful. I already have the spirit of violence in me as I acquired from my ancestors so it wasn't hard for me to get a lot of reinforcements from my guardian demons (acquired from generational curses). As I retaliated, my pride kept on growing stronger and higher than Mt. Everest. Still, I had a best friend despite all my weaknesses. Like any abusive relationships, there was always someone willing to take that abuse – that's the positive side of bad. Psychologist would refer to these people as masochist. But understanding God's language now, they are not. They are chosen by God to help bring people back to his fold.

Despite my bad behavior, Simone, my college best friend never abandoned me. She took a chance when nobody ever did. She stood by me and became my real-life guardian angel. I wasn't used to having someone believed in me, believing that there was something good within me or cared for me in that capacity that I felt threatened. I was scared that I was beginning to care for someone I was afraid of losing. Like any coward would do, I tried my best to drive her away before she dropped me for another friend. I just turned 18 years old then. She actually helped me plan my debut just a month prior to her death. I was too old to behave in such a way – but I did anyways. I blamed myself for her death thinking that if I had been kinder to her or if I had not cut her off the day prior to her death, then maybe, she wouldn't have rode on that boat. I would have consistently bugged her over the phone and kept her at shore. I used to be haunted by feelings of regret that perhaps if I were a better friend, I would have taught her how to swim so she wouldn't have drowned. I have been a competitive swimmer for years and wondered if I could have done something. It took me a while to accept that there was nothing I could have done even if I turned back the time. What made it so traumatic was that, all throughout summer that year, she was always making sure I wake up in time for summer class. She would always bring extra set of yellow paper for me for daily exams. I became extremely dependent on her. We slept with my two other classmates in my room one afternoon, while we wait for our evening session class, and I had a nightmare. It was a three-episode nightmare. The first episode was that I ran over someone. The second episode had the name of my college crush, and the last episode was an image of the ocean – it was so still. But it was the episode that I totally woke up crying. I was so scared and I couldn't understand why. Simone was holding my hand as she was comforting me. She always come up with funny jokes and funny interpretation of my dreams. Since then, when I take my afternoon naps, she would be holding my hand. There were two other classmates that sleep with us but Simone would only be holding my hand just so I could sleep and I won't get a nightmare. True enough, I didn't have nightmares anymore during my afternoon naps.

As summer was coming to a close, and so were our classes, I experienced sleep paralysis one night. I saw a silhouette of a man coming inside the front door. I could see him from my own bedroom door that was partially open. My mind was extremely conscious. I couldn't move. I couldn't say anything. I was literally paralyzed until the man was coming closer to me that I screamed in my head then "boom" I woke up. I was so scared. I went to my mother's room to sleep.

I woke up late. Simone didn't call me. When I got to school, we had our morning exam and I didn't have my yellow paper. I had to scramble and fortunately, I was able to source one. Simone looked disturbed as well. She seemed edgy. I was angry with her for not waking me up and not having any yellow paper for me.

After class, I stormed out of the room. Simone ran after me until we got into the parking lot. I yelled at her. Telling her how she was always pretending to be good when she wasn't. There were so many things I said to her that were very horrible. I was literally accusing her. I was also jealous of her goodness. I was jealous of her kindness because no matter what I do, I couldn't seem to be kind. I was jealous of her patience because I don't seem to have any. She cried and I felt so guilty. She explained to me why she didn't wake me because she had a nightmare that night. She dreamt of being in the ocean with sharks all around her. I also told her I had a "bangungot" in Filipino to mean "sleep paralysis". We settled but I was already decided on pushing her away. I was so disturbed that I needed her so much. I just wanted to keep my distance from her. I was already very scared of losing her. I didn't want to be dependent on her anymore. I distanced myself from her until the end of summer.

Then one Saturday before her passing, we talked about them burying a relative in Dumanjug. I think it was her paternal grandmother who slipped and just died. I was still distant from her. I decided, I'll keep my distance until class starts which was already in a week. We drove to Ayala Center Cebu Mall and while all my classmates who hitched a ride with me left ahead, Simone refused to leave me. I said, "You can go ahead Simone". But she insisted and said, "No, I will never leave you April". I just shrugged it off as if I didn't care.

As I went to hang out with my old High School friends, I bid goodbye to Simone because she said she was going home. It's like that moment stopped for me. I wanted so much to hug her and tell her "Thank you for being such a good friend to me". She was smiling at me- with her angelic smile. And I decided to hold myself back, and thought, we will always have next week. I'll make it up to her then. I maintained looking nonchalant and said so coldly, "Bye Simone". I didn't even say "See you next week!". She left with a sad look on her face. I really couldn't get that image of her face out of my mind. She looked very sad.

Then the following day, I went out of town on a long drive with my high school friends – I was with my high school best friend, Jobe. I was so confident that I was happy. We had fun that day. I was thinking of Simone and I said to myself, "See? I have my old friends too. You can be with your other friends and I'll be just fine". While we attended the last evening mass that Sunday, I got a text message from Melissa, who was also Simone's former classmate in Highschool. Melissa asked if I have heard of Simone because she heard she met a "fatal" accident. At that time, my vocabulary wasn't as developed yet so I didn't fully realize that fatal means "death". The entire time while I was in mass, I was imagining that Simone got into a car accident and when I visit her in the hospital, she will tell me I am the super best friend she ever had, that she doesn't want other friends but me and we will be best friends forever.

As soon as we got home, I called her. She always answered the phone. Always. There was never a time where I called her number that she didn't pick up. That night, it wasn't her voice. It was an unfamiliar voice. I asked, "Hi, where is Simone?" and the person on the other line said, "Simone died, April". Somehow, her cousin knew who I was because I always call Simone. Upon hearing that Simone had died, I jolted that I hit my head on the bed. I dropped the phone. I was kicking and screaming on the floor crying my heart out. I felt like a headless chicken. I called again and ask where Simone was. Her cousin told me she's in the morgue. At that time, we could still enter the morgue. I went to Cebu Doctor's Hospital Morgue. There she was. Lying on the bed. Lifeless. It wasn't Simone anymore. I couldn't feel her anymore. She was hard and cold. She was gone. The finality of it was just too much for me to handle and all I could recall over and over again was the day before where I could have hugged her so tight had I known it was going to be my last day with her. I had a nervous breakdown. I couldn't stop crying, I was inconsolable. My mom was getting so worried for me and told me I am going crazy. I locked myself in my room. I didn't want to see anyone. I get panic attacks – always roll calling my dad and my mom. Every single minute of the day. I would call them nonstop to check if they were okay. When I went to her wake, I talked to her maternal grandmother, who told me Simone always spoke so fondly of me. And that day, Simone kept asking her if she was a good person. That again broke my heart. I knew she was asking that because of me – because of what I said to her when I got mad at her in the parking lot. I felt so guilty that I was the last person that hurt her. But looking on hindsight, it was a good thing that she was examining her conscience – the things she did wrong before she died because she would have been able to ask God for forgiveness, knowing Simone. Those questions she asked her grandmother significantly helped prepare her soul for death. As for me though, the guilt stayed with me for over 20 years.

I recovered from the loss after several years of mourning. I wrote her a letter that I left in her coffin the day she was buried and promised that I would always give everyone a chance – no matter what. I kept that promise except that over the years, I came up with a few disclaimers.

But what did Simone's kindness and willingness to stand by me even if I was so cruel to her did to me? Her authenticity and holiness as a human being led to my conversion. Her death, led to my conversion. Her death, literally forced me to transform. Her death, literally led me to put a huge dent on my pride. It is important to emphasize that conversion is a very long process. It just doesn't happen overnight, in a year but over a long period of time depending on our spiritual support system; and degree of inherited spirits infesting our souls and our bloodlines. Conversion also isn't a linear process. It oscillates, which I'll cover on another chapter. I actually just realized that Simone was my personal saint. I became one of her spiritual fruits. All her efforts to love me weren't wasted because her compassion towards me had transformed me. Simone's parents are actually both devout Catholics. I have witnessed the level of integrity they passed on to their children. Back in architecture school, we had an engineering class, where 95% of the students failed. Simone and I were one of them. The professor back then was quite notorious as his way of earning additional money from his students. So, one day, the offer came. I was so lucky because I had Simone. The rest of my classmates were willing to pay just to pass. My brothers encouraged me to do it – because they claimed it was just a class. But thanks to Simone's parents, they refused. They were willing to let Simone fail, and to think she was a *Dean's Lister.* It would have left a permanent mark on her record. I followed Simone. I couldn't do it also. There was a part of me that just couldn't do it. Lo and behold, the professor gave us an opportunity to pass. He gave us two difficult problems that we needed to demonstrate how we will solve it. And by God's grace, Simone and I did it. Separately of course. We were both given two different sets of problems to solve and we both did it, effortlessly too. We were failing it because of the pressure we were putting ourselves into that we couldn't think of the solution during the exam. But it's different when we were made to explain our solution because it forces us to get a hold of ourselves and actually think. Although there was a part of me that always suspected that Simone intentionally failed her exam so I won't feel left alone. All other classmates failed too but I felt that Simone intentionally failed that class for me.

Before coming to New York, I would watch <u>CNN</u> until the wee hours of the morning and fantasized about saving the world. In my own way, I've tried to do something about seeing little kids knocking on my car door window to ask for a coin. I never liked to give money because I knew that they wouldn't get to keep it. What I did at first was bought a pack of candies. A friend of mine later reprimanded me that I was causing them more harm than good because they will have to deal with a sore tooth and they wouldn't be able to afford to go to a dentist. I later decided to buy packs of biscuits instead and that worked out just perfectly. On Christmas days, I would drive around several street-children locations and gave out sandwiches. I used to do this with my cousin and a friend. It felt really good but trust me, the feeling was selfish. It just made me feel good that I didn't have to see hungry, malnourished faces when I gave them food (even if realistically speaking, the biscuits just helped very little). It really bothered me a lot and still does. Every time a child knocks on my car door window and they look so awfully hungry and tired, it quenched my heart to a point of frustration at my helplessness to change this reality– and it just haunt me all day long.

After college, when most of my friends were planning their weddings, my goal was to earn my first million (in pesos). Not that I didn't try to get myself married, but the right one just never came along. I had my first *"official"* boyfriend when I was 22 years old and it was a fairly platonic relationship. He was a very good man. He was the best friend of my uncle-cousin. All of them, including my ex-fling belong in the same circle of friends. My uncle's father was the youngest first cousin of my grandmother, and it so happens that my uncle and I have the same age. We were more cousins in real life so I'll refer to him as my cousin. Though my relationship with my boyfriend didn't last very long of course, barely two months, but he was my first real date in my life. He took me to watch Miss Saigon at the Cultural Center of the Philippines, with a rose to start with. He was very intelligent and tall too. It was literally me who closed the deal with him by acting jealous, and asking him if he had a girlfriend, and he said no. I asked him again if he doesn't have a girlfriend, he denied it again. I looked sad and said, oh Ok, so you don't have a girlfriend. That's when he finally realized I wanted to be his girlfriend. He then said, yes, I have a girlfriend now.

It was that easy and I wasn't scared. It felt quite natural. The problem was, I was so excited to finally sleep with him like most of my friends from high school. Though I was Catholic, I was already curious about sex because of my cyber-ex something that got me into trouble in college. I was already an Architect then and I thought, perhaps this time, its okay for me to try it. Though I grew up in a Catholic school, I don't think my school was very effective in emphasizing why sex must be preserve for marriage. Because if only I understood back then the harm sex does to our soul if not protected by the Sacrament of Matrimony (in a way that I understand now), and gain that awareness of what it actually means when our soul is harmed, I would have stayed a virgin until I got married. Perhaps, things would have been different for me.

Prior to meeting my boyfriend, I had a fling while I was reviewing for the board exam in Manila (I was very insecure and uncertain of my life then) and that guy happened to be my ex-boyfriend's friend too. I was literally a fling. Like a booty call without the actually booty act. Just up to 3rd base. Though I remained a virgin, the spiritual contamination had been significant. If we can get contaminated just by sitting next to them or talking to them, how much more when you share a kiss, or any form of intimacy, even without sex. Sex is the worst because your souls would be tied. When you separate, your souls would be torn apart causing so many deep spiritual wounds. But upon meeting my boyfriend thru my cousin, I forgot the other guy. At least briefly. He was never serious anyways so I didn't take him seriously too. But my boyfriend wouldn't touch or kiss me when we were alone. I broke up with him literally because I didn't think he was into me. I was already contaminated with the spirit of lust. He only kissed me when in public. That confused me so much, only to realize later, like two or three years after why he wouldn't touch me then. He said because he respected me so much. He was already seeing me as his potential wife. By the time he told me that, he was already too late. I already gave myself away to that fling who came back to me six months after I broke up with my boyfriend. That fling felt sorry for how he treated me, which I really didn't care much for at that time. For a moment, I was torn if I should tell my ex-boyfriend what transpired between me and his friend. I had a choice to keep this unofficial relationship from my ex-boyfriend who was offering me marriage. He was just asking for time for him to earn his way to becoming self-sufficient so that he can be a good provider. However, my conscience simply could not handle it. I literally broke it off with the ex-fling before my ex-boyfriend called me up because I felt sick to my stomach. It's like I lost a part of me that I could no longer get back. I cried because it didn't feel right. I was literally mourning. I told my ex-boyfriend the truth and he was very angry with himself. He was blaming himself that I destroyed myself because of him. I was already stolen before we even broke up while we were in Boracay that first month we just got together. The ex-fling was there and he was tempting me to cheat. My ex-boyfriend chose to stay in Subic in order to avoid the temptation. He was so much of a gentleman. Fortunately, I didn't cheat — at least not physically. But mentally? The demons have already managed to infest in my thoughts. I had the will power to say no then but it was only a matter of time. The enemy knew they will get me eventually. And they did.

I really thought I was in love with my ex-fling but I was merely using *love* as an excuse to justify my mistake. He became one of my excuses because I wanted to leave for New York. I followed him. Although, it was more of the fantasy I was after, because like I said, I gave myself to him but I regretted doing so. I felt so extremely sick- I cannot emphasize that enough. But I didn't want to lose the fantasy of being in love. In the back of my mind, I was hoping I would end up marrying him but I didn't do anything to at least make contact while I was in New York. The mistake most people have when they think of marriage was that it's the validation of a happy ending. I did imagine marrying him but I never could imagine being married to anyone. I used to share that mindset too. My pride and belief in fate just wouldn't let me do it. I've always been a hopeless romantic. I wanted fate to bring us together and not me forcing the situation. I just thought I would help fate by being in the same vicinity as him (Yes, I was aware New York was so huge but so is the world). However, everything changed when I moved to I-House. I moved to I-House in December of 2005. At that time, I was seeing John, my classmate at my university, where I was enrolled for my master's program. He was very sweet. He helped me moved in. He would pick me up to and from I-House. I thought we were already dating. While we were in the elevator that first night, I moved into I-House, I noticed a very handsome – princely looking European man. I remembered this because he was the Danish man I fell in love with approximately a month after. This Danish man was also the one who reminded me where he first saw me. I was flying out to San Francisco one evening, and it was very cold. It was less than zero in New York City. John suddenly called me because he had a Christmas present, he wanted to give me. He walked to I House just to give me that gift. I never ever recall anyone giving me a gift in that manner. Not with so much effort. I felt so grateful to him. I invited him to my room – literally, without malice in my mind. We kissed but it was only up to there. He was a gentleman like my ex-boyfriend. And I hugged him very tight before I left for San Francisco. I was so happy and grateful that he would do that for me. It was such a big deal for me because I never really get any gifts like that. I had a very simple measure of happiness it's probably because I have been so deprived of it. It wasn't more about the gift but more of the effort. While on the plane to San Francisco, I suddenly felt scared. I literally felt so scared that I may already be in a relationship. I was literally getting cold feet. It was the same feeling I felt when I thought that the ex-fling, I was following to New York from the Philippines, has got me into a relationship with him. I literally went crazy. I panicked. I literally got a panic attack. I remember calling him all the way to New York asking him if we were already in a relationship. I don't recall his answer but I was scaring him. I think he ended up saying its better we will stop talking to each other. And I recall accepting it immediately. Of course, I felt extremely rejected. But later, he called me back every so often until something eventually happened between the two of us when I travelled to New York. He was very persistent and I also prepared for it too. I was taking birth control pills even when I was still a virgin. I realized later how much damaged I caused my soul. That time, the demons finally succeeded in devouring me.

I was on the plane to San Francisco when I got scared of what I might be starting with John. I had time to relax and while I was staying with my grade school classmate then, where I kept hearing about her complicated relationship with her boyfriend, I started yearning for one. I called John, who never called me back since I left San Francisco. We talked briefly, and he said, "Talk you later, April". I literally waited for him to call me back but he never did. When I returned to New York, I was asking him why he didn't call me back when he said he will call me. He said he didn't tell me he will call back. I said, "you said you will talk to me later!?" Then John laughed. He said, "Later" is just an expression but it didn't mean it refers to a particular time. Talking about cultural differences, huh? Since then, he was teaching me the New York lingo and idiomatic expressions. I did ask him if we were together already. He told me, he liked me so much but he would very much love to continue seeing me as his friend. I was extremely heartbroken but I accepted it gracefully. We remained friends. I literally was truthful of just being friends with him.

I have this tendency to think of things with finality but it must be the romantic in me. I loved the idea of falling in love. I would design ways of how I want to fall and then plan on how I hope it will end. But in this particular case, I didn't want nor plan to fall in love (because I thought I was still in love with my ex-fling). Yet I did and the feeling then felt so new to me. I have never felt more scared in my life. It was a different kind of scared. It was a similar feeling to how I felt with Simone. The timing was also impeccable since it was also a moment wherein, I was still trying to find stability with my life in New York City. I was still unsure of where I was going especially the need to find a potential employer that would sponsor me (it was still my first year so I had a long way to go then). I was an intern at the United Nations Capital Development Fund (UNCDF) at that time. My money was literally running out.

The guy I was falling in love with was the Danish guy. I met him one evening during an Eastern European Cultural Hour. This was the night after I was rejected by John. I was adamant on finding someone. I was following a certain guy from Luxembourg, whom I thought looked so much like Brad Pitt. But that night, during the show, my friend Michael who came with me to the show, suddenly begged to go. Then that Danish guy swooped in next to me.

He was really very beautiful. Very handsome that I wasn't interested. Because he was too beautiful, I immediately rejected the idea that he would be interested in me. I decided already. So, I was just very casual with him. Little did I know that he was following me around. I was carefree because I was heartbroken. I just needed to have fun and be jolly, - be pretentious. I can be very good at that back in the day. I can fake being happy if I really wanted to. It takes a lot of effort for me to start but once I'm on a roll, I'm on a roll. I wanted to go to this *Community Weekend* getaway in Tacoma, New York but because I have this attitude that usually repelled certain people, I was excluded. My floor mates all made it but me. But that night, after seeing me with the Danish guy, whom I didn't know was already flirting with me, I suddenly got called that I'm in. I was so happy and told the Danish guy I don't know what to bring. Even though I was no longer a virgin but I really was still quite innocent. I was completely oblivious to a guy's sexual innuendos. When the Danish guy told me that he had the list in his room, I was so quick to accept his offer to accompany him. I didn't realize that it meant something else. So, when I got into his room, I saw his IPAQ, which at that time was very high tech for me but compared to now, it's a very primitive version of a tablet. And I was a geek. I am really a techy. I sat on his bed while I was inspecting his IPAQ, when he started touching my legs. Even though he was very beautiful, I wasn't really into him because like I said, I decided that I am not. I can be very firm when I decide on something. I decided to leave and he tried to kiss me. I turned a cheek and said, it's not a good idea because I am not sober. He knew I was lying but he was kind enough to let me go. I felt like I had the "longest hair" ever – an English translation of a Tagalog expression, "ang haba ng hair ko" to mean I am feeling conceited. I felt good rejecting a very handsome and beautiful man. Though it wasn't my intention but I felt pretty damn good then.

The following morning, I was confident that I have an edge over him. I thought he would be very embarrassed because I rejected him. I was shocked when I saw him. He was literally surrounded with a flock of beautiful women from the United Colors of Benetton – simply put, from diverse backgrounds. They were like models. Very beautiful and they were all following him around. I started to get curious on who this guy really was. All I knew of him was his name and that he was Danish. While I looked at my crew- oh well, no offense, but they were geeks like me. You know, people who are just unique with our very specific quirks that geeks usually have - more on the less cool side. While the Danish guy was with the super cool gang. I tried to catch his attention several times but he really wouldn't look at me. Until that evening, I decided to sit right next to him. That broke him. So, when he asked me to hang out with him in the community center, I knew what he wanted from me so I went with him. I wasn't really into him. I was just lonely and I didn't want to feel alone. I can do the usual foreplay; though I don't really enjoy it but it's something I can do mechanically. And that's what we were doing. While in the middle of doing that, he blurted out that, "maybe I have a girlfriend". As soon as I heard that, I stopped. I really have a very strong aversion to cheating. I said, I have to go. He asked why. And I told him very firmly that we live in one house, and I don't ever want to be involved in a conflict with another woman in the house. I emphasized that we were a family in the house and will be for a long time so I don't want to do anything to jeopardize that. While we were going out of the community center, he offered to take me to my cabin but I told him I'm a big girl and I will be just fine. I was treating him like a little boy. I was shooing him away. As I was walking to my cabin on that super snowy night, I suddenly got pulled by the Danish guy and he kissed me in a way that he would suck my soul out of me. I totally didn't see that coming. I resisted at first and then I melted. I didn't realize that what we see in the movies with a scene like that can really happen in real life. I was dumbfounded when he let me go. It was like I was floating on *Cloud 9*. I was still processing what happened in my mind and when I got to my cabin, my friend then, Lisa, was asking me if I saw some cute guys. I was like lost in my thoughts because of that kiss. She then mentioned that he found the Danish guy to be very handsome. That's when I woke up from my dreamlike state. I ended up describing to her everything that happened.

I thought, that was the end of it. I was literally avoiding the Danish guy because he was still in a relationship. When we were in the elevator, he would literally grab and kiss me, similar to that snowy evening. My eyes would get so smoky – and I felt like I had a fever. For sure we had chemistry. I cannot say if it was lust. I think God was trying to get me to break down my barriers. I remember always resisting that Danish guy. I literally would avoid making conversations with him. I literally would stay as far away from him but I would seek him out from a distance. He would always make my day complete just by seeing him from a distance. He was an excellent debater too. The more I listen to him, the more I was growing more in love with him – it was a different kind of feeling. There was a tenderness I feel for him each day I seek him out. I later heard he finally broke up with his girlfriend. And during All Nations, I cooked *chicken adobo* to be sold for the community. I cooked it all by myself and I was doing it all for him. I was thinking in my mind, if he only knew that I cooked all this for him, would he appreciate it? Of course, all those dedications were just all in my mind. I never told him. Then that night, when we sold the chicken, He bought the chicken and even complained to me how expensive it was since we were selling them at $4 each. So much for me thinking that he would know I was cooking it for him after I sold it to him, right? But I still thought he would ask me out. I tend to overthink that way too and not realize that he doesn't know how I feel. I can be really thick sometimes. I literally tend to assume he knew what was on my mind the entire time. I had a similarity with a character in a film, *the Secret Life of Walter Mitty,* who tend to zone off with his imagination. Instead, I saw him with his very beautiful ex-girlfriend from Azerbaijan. Her beauty was totally out of this world. If he was beautiful? She was magical. I really felt so insecure. I saw him holding her hand, as if begging her to come back to him. I went to my room and cried. I cried my heart out. The following weeks, I would see him and he would still come to me. I think he had one of his friends be-friended me so he can have information on me. I would know how to bait him to come to me too despite me thinking he might be with his ex. Somehow, I had the feeling that I have an edge over her – basically because he never really got me. I knew about the power of unfulfilled desires. That was probably why I resisted so much so I can maintain my power over him. He was also very good at reading body language. He was really very intelligent and his intelligence was precisely what made me so attracted to him more than his beauty.

Just a week prior to his graduation, he asked me out – as friends. We had lunch – Dutch style. We talked – it didn't feel like a date. But the attraction was definitely there. We even watched a movie with a group of people and the next thing I knew, he took a big bite of my upper arm that literally bruised for days. I was so naive that when we hung out with his friends, they were asking what happened to my arm, and I grumpily said, "He friggin' bit me all of a sudden while we were watching Harold & Kumar went to White Castle!". His friends looked at each other and laughed. They said, 'Wow that sounds like someone is struggling with suppressed desires". I was quite embarrassed. While I may be quite open and literally very transparent with everything in my life (my circle of friends would often refer to me as a "pilot" because I keep announcing what I have done and what I will do next), but I actually prefer to keep my relationships "ultra" private. At least while it is still on going. The only time I talk about it is when I am so heartbroken and I simply cannot handle to keep it in my thoughts with the never-ending questions of "why, why, why" and all the "what-ifs" but I am careful to avoid mentioning their names.

One day, because I knew he will be leaving soon, I asked my friend to give him the Alchemist book I had in my room to be given to him. It came with a very long note – and I can be really romantic with my notes. I love letter writing. I expressed to him all my repressed emotions. I thought that I will never see him again. To my surprise, he came knocking on my door that same night and left me a note under my door. I refused to go out of course. But the next morning, he got me. Literally. He was the second guy I was intimate with. Right after that, I cried. I realized I was so in love with him and all I could think of was that he will be gone soon. While most women would probably fantasize of having a future with a guy like that, I did the opposite. I started creating a story in my mind that he was just using me as a notch on his belt. I was really quite cruel with myself. I had all those horror thoughts in my head that a guy only wants sex and since he got me, it's over. But he didn't want to leave. He wanted to have breakfast. I was already going crazy. Literally crying my heart out. I was inconsolable. Any guy would have been scared. I scared him – I was asking him to leave. John, on the other hand, came to my rescue. He had no awareness that I was already falling in love with someone from the house. I wasn't thinking that he had feelings for me since we agreed we were just friends. I decided to just hang out with John. One night, my cousin asked me to go out and I saw my ex-fling. He was single then and I realized, I never really loved him. I remember having feelings for him but at that moment, I could not recall the feelings anymore. Instead of feeling relieved, I was extremely depressed. The following morning, I called the Danish guy and told him I need to speak with him. Fortunately, he gave me the time. So, I went to his room. I told him how alone I felt seeing my ex-fling and realize I didn't have feelings for him anymore. I told him he was the reason I moved to New York. And now, there seems to be no reason at all. The Danish guy hugged me. Sincerely hugged me. I thanked him for his kindness in hearing me out and I wished him luck with his life in Beijing. I really felt at peace with myself. If he had let me go then, I would have been fine. But the most romantic thing happened when I came home that day from work.

As I was entering I-House, I forgot that I left my clothes in the drycleaner. So instead of going in, I didn't. The Danish guy was by the door and he thought I was avoiding him. I literally didn't see him. By the time I got back to I-House, he was hiding behind the door and I noticed there was someone following me. I turned around and realized it was him. For some reason, I felt excitedly scared. Scared in the sense at how extremely romantic that moment was. He literally ran after me. While in the elevator, he begged me if he could talk to me in a public setting. And so, I agreed.

He was showing me his place in Denmark. I was confused. Somehow, we got into a conversation where he told me,

"You are so risk-averse April, you live your life with a checklist that you don't have room for the unknown and a lot of wonderful things can happen when you don't live on a checklist". And I recall telling him, "I am very scared. I can only trust myself and in the end, I am the only one who can pick myself up". Then he told me, "Sometimes in life, we have to gamble. Because love is a gamble". Remember when I said I have *ADHD*? The thing with that is, it's very slow processing. Everything that he said only dawned on me years after. There was an opportunity for us to be together that afternoon but when I was in his room, John called me. And in front of the Danish guy, I lied to John and told him I was on my way to my room. I suddenly noticed the change in his eyes. From very kind eyes to not so kind eyes. He didn't seek me out after that. And I let it be. I applied to an International Field Work program in Hong Kong that summer. I was hoping it would be enough to make me forget him. I was living and working in Hong Kong for two months. A few months after, the Danish guy was already in Beijing. As I was growing more and more in love with him, I was growing more and more depressed. I was no longer fun to hang around with. I was literally causing conflicts with female friends. I get extremely prideful. I got so troublesome. I was a magnet for trouble. When I went back to New York the following semester, I finally processed everything I experienced with Danish guy. Instead of me forgetting him, I was growing more in love especially because I wasn't really able to share a relationship with him. All we ever had was stolen moments. The sad thing was, the romance was building up in my head. I kept on fantasizing on the memories – on how romantic it was. I totally forgot God by this time. God was no longer in the equation. It was just him, my loneliness, my misery, my future – my dark, depressing future. I got a job and thought I'll forget him. I didn't. The following year, I always travel to another country each time I go home to Cebu, and at that time, I was planning to visit him in Beijing. I really missed him so much. So, I messaged him and he was kind enough to offer that I stay in his apartment. Of course, I told our mutual friend, who reminded me if I am certain and I'll be just fine if he sleeps with me again. And I said, "What? No. I just want to see him and perhaps find closure?" But our mutual friend probably had a better idea of my intentions that she just blatantly told me, "A guy is a guy April. He will always take whatever it is that you are offering". I got so hurt and messaged the Danish guy that I hope he understand I have no plans of sleeping with him and would sincerely appreciate it if he won't try to seduce me. I had this very good outcome planned in my mind that he would simply respect it and we will be friends like "John". I imagined he would accept it as gracefully as how I gracefully I accepted John's rejection of me.

But the Danish guy got mad. He said he would be lying if he said he won't try to sleep with me and that he didn't need any more friends since he got plenty of friends. That hurt me so much. He then proceeded to telling me that it's probably better that we won't talk or chat with each other in a couple of years then perhaps by then, we can *just* be friends. He was true to his words. He never contacted me again and I thought that was over for us. I was extremely heartbroken because I was just willing to settle being *just* friends with him and even that, he couldn't even give to me. I thought if we will just be friends, like how I was with John, I could eventually adjust to the idea that we will just be friends and the *attraction* or the *love* feeling will just die a natural death. I was extremely unhappy already and I just wanted to be freed from that kind of unhappiness. To make things worse, when I went to Beijing, I literally saw him seated behind me at an outdoor restaurant. He was with a Chinese woman and he was literally caressing her back. I could see it from where I was. I knew he saw me but I also pretended not to see him.

On top of this heartache, there were so many limitations of being an international student. We were not allowed to accept paid employment while we were in school during the first year or in some special cases, we were but it came with a lot of red tapes, approvals, and other immigration requirements, etc. My father at that time was not supporting me (since I went against his wishes) so I was supporting myself via student loans. Fortunately, my sister co-signed the loan with me and even though I had zero credit score, I was granted a $30,000 student loan. Regardless, I kept myself busy with internships while I attended class in the evening. While it was popular for most foreign non-immigrants and international students to work as waitresses, bartenders or do manual labor to make ends meet, I always saw the wisdom in building my resume doing unpaid internships in order to gain a credible New York work experience. Even my sister didn't quite agree with me then as she would rather, I look for a job that will pay for my loans like earning a $4-$8/hour job at McDonalds. I didn't listen of course and I'm quite glad that I was stubborn since all my sacrifices paid off in the end because I was able to get a job offer as an Environmental and Building Management Consultant with a $45,000 entry level salary plus benefits in Midtown Manhattan two years after despite not having a Master's degree.

Fast forward to 2007, I saw the Danish guy again, heading to the exit door in I-House. He was heading towards 125th street train station because he turned left. Or that's what I thought. I decided to walk to 116th street expecting that the likelihood of us seeing each other given that we were on two different stations was very low. To my surprise, as soon as I went down the stairs, I saw him from a distance. I quickly hid behind the column. I really didn't think he saw me. The next thing I knew, he was calling my name from behind me. I panicked. I thought – should I pretend not to hear him? Maybe if I wait a little, he will just go away. He didn't. He called my name again. I turned around and pretended to be surprised. There he went again with his sarcastic grin – because he knew I was lying. He started saying, "April, about what I said to you before…." – I decided to cut off him and said, "Don't worry about it, its water under the bridge". For me, it was because I really couldn't hate him. I loved him so much to hate him. I just didn't know what to do with him at that time because I was so nervous seeing him so unexpectedly.

Then the train arrived and we were standing across each other. He was looking at me again – in the same way he used to look at me when we were left alone before. My knees were shaking and I just couldn't maintain my gaze. He was trying to start a conversation but I was just too nervous so when my stop came, I just bid him goodbye and left. And then that was it. I was haunted by that train ride for over 10 years. I kept on rehashing the memory – what if I talked to him a little bit more? Asked him about himself? What if I just took a day off that day and spent it with him? But I would never know.

I realized that I came to New York so I can pursue something big – something much bigger than myself. The ex-fling was just an excuse should I fail or in case I was feeling unsure of myself. I felt I had a calling. I wanted to make a difference in this world. I have been told that I am a dreamer and have been for a long time. I've always refused to see the impossibility and always resisted the notion that my dreams can't come true. Although my life growing up has never been easy but I've always looked up. I always get to compare myself to others who appear as though their lives had been easier than mine. The notion that my life is not easy seems to be a comfort to me in the sense that I feel as though I've gotten past the hurdles in my life and I am still standing. A friend once said, "Don't worry when the door closes; just watch out when God raises the roof". I'm saying OK, I'm watching out for it.

What made me go to a Psychic?

One afternoon sometime in late 2006, at this time, I was already expelled. I was strolling along SOHO district in Manhattan, I think it was across Bloomingdales, when I saw a "Psychic" sign. I decided to pass by it. Suddenly, a woman approached me. She was smiling and she called me by my first name. I was surprised and asked how she knew, and she said "Your spirit told my spirit your name. Come up, let's talk". So, I went up and the first thing I saw was a woman crying. I felt icky. I felt a darkness inside her quite modern office. We sat on her office (yeah, it was an office, almost like a conference room and her service was to offer psychic consultation) and she asked me to list down my birthdate before she can begin.

I said, "Why? What for?" I was feeling doubtful that she might use it for identity theft. She then said she needed me to tell her. I said, "why don't you ask your spirit to ask my spirit my birthdate?" Then I stood up and decided to leave. She tried to stop me and said, "A woman in your family is going to get you killed! You will die! My spirit said you need help!". And I said, "I don't care! I am leaving" And I left.

Allow me to walk you back in the spring of 2006 where I met a Filipina friend who just moved into I-House. She was from Davao. I was the resident fellow on an all women floor. I was already working, but I managed to still stay in I-House. I have at least another year before I am no longer eligible to live there. She came to me one evening to express a concern that while on the subway, a lady came up to her telling her that something bad will happen to her. For some reason, she engaged the lady who was psychic. She told me the story on how she went to her place and gave her $600 and was asking for more. She told me she told her uncle about it who also knew about occult stuff and it was finally over. I was so confounded at how ridiculous it was that she believed the psychic. I just brushed this aside. I never gave it a second thought.

Fast forward to spring of 2007, I was growing more and more depressed. One evening, while on the bus going home to I-House, I saw a "psychic sign" on a two-story building. I got off the bus and the next thing I knew, I was already knocking on the psychic's door. The first thing I told her was, "I need your help. A psychic lady I met the last year said I will die and I don't know what to do." I followed everything she told me and on the last day, the day of reckoning, she asked me to buy a dozen eggs on the deli below her apartment. She asked me to write something on the black cloth with my intentions. And she asked me for money in my bank account. She wanted all of it. But I decided to just give her $600. I don't know then why I decided on $600. She was baiting me that I have more and I said, that's all I have. She told me that if the egg was clear when she breaks it, it means I'm already cleared but if there is something in it, then I just got cleared. Either way, she wins. Either way, her ways worked. That's what she was implying. So true enough, she picked a rotten egg. After that, I felt really uneasy. I felt like I did something that was just simply so wrong. I told the psychic that I needed to tell someone. She warned me that if I do, the curse will come back twice as bad. She said that if I didn't come to her, I would have committed suicide because of the woman in my family. I told her, I want to confess to a priest because it was the only logical thing, I can do being Catholic. She threatened me that "priests" are only human. I recall telling her, "I don't care! No one is stronger than God1" I said that with my eyes closed. I was adamant on confessing it to God. When I opened my eyes, I could see the fear in her eyes. She wanted to return the money – but I hesitated. And with that slight hesitation – the enemy immediately got me. Pride of not wanting the money back (even if I needed it more than ever), and fear that what if she was right. All my bravado on God just all went away. It didn't hold. But one thing was certain that day – I decided I will never ever go back to a psychic ever again.

Shortly after that, an idea came into my mind that I will start a nonprofit organization called **Omnilogy Inc** – it was named after my thesis. It was my way for me to keep my thesis alive. I had that notion that it will be stolen and might see it get published under a different name. But I truly felt guided. I was so motivated. I wrote my *Mission & Vision* and it felt so good. It was primarily focused on promoting *One Humanity – where everyone, everywhere matters.* That was my slogan. My background music then was John Lennon's "Imagine". Of course, at that time, I didn't realize it was an atheist song. Somehow, I didn't meet any hurdles. I even got a silent benefactor from the Phil-NY Junior Chamber community in New York. My non-profit exactly had the same tax-exempt status as International House, New York. I got the approval in just six months. I gathered all my network from I-House who were all very supportive of me. I got them to volunteer to do a music residency in Cebu for underprivileged kids in Cebu. We would have a project every month, sometimes two events. It was very successful at that time and we were getting a lot of visibility. I teamed up with many organizations. Collaboration at that time was none existent but since I didn't have much resources to work with, it was the only resource I pretty much have. I have the network of the artist – internationally renowned ones, so I approached the local Art's Council, of which one of the board members was my professor whom I used to be really afraid of back in college. I remember when I approached him when I came back from New York, I told him, "Sir, I have met David Rockefeller and many more like him in New York, whom I talk to casually, but until now, I am still nervous to talk to you". That broke the ice. He laughed. He supported me all throughout. I remember organizations from Manila inviting me and my artists to perform there – but at that time, I was more focused on empowering Cebu. I was driven to bring Cebu to the world because I felt very much discriminated by my professor. I really tend to think so big sometimes even when I was literally working from nothing. I had nothing but just my guts – and my family money. My family never realized that we had money until they were spending for my projects. I had no income then. I had no job. I was not earning at all. I was living off my credit card and savings from my two-year work stint in New York. I had a pretty huge credit line with an impeccable credit score.

My annual budget for my projects was no less than one million pesos/year (approx. $20,000). I had to pay for my volunteers' airfares, accommodations and local tours. My first volunteer was an incredible pianist from Israel, who played for the Berlin Philharmonic Orchestra at that time. He was extremely gifted. We were not even close but for the life of me, I don't know why he agreed to fly to Cebu, twice. To do a fundraiser for my non-profit, which of course didn't earn very much because back in 2008, philanthropy was not quite on the social menu yet. Omnilogy was a fledgling organization. But in the three years in operation, we have taught several street-children and children in the mountain barangays how to play a musical instrument, where it would normally just be available in elite schools. Their instructors were world-class performers. Literally. We would hold recitals for our participating students – there were a few gifted ones who were homeschooled. One of them, a promising violinist, excelled and was later accepted to Brown University. Another had joined the Philharmonic orchestra in Europe as a cellist. The entire time, when people asked me why I am doing this charity, I would always correct them – I would use to be quick to say, it's not charity, its philanthropy. I had a strong aversion to anything that sounded religious at that time. I didn't realize yet that I totally didn't have faith anymore until we collaborated with a Buddhist Temple in Cebu, as a potential concert venue that I actually heard myself say, "*I think I will be a Buddhist*." The inclination was definitely there given that my grandfather was pure Chinese and was practicing Buddhism until he died. I just said it but I never actually did it. My mom would always scold me because I refused to go to church. I remember her telling me, "*April, if you stop going to church, you will really starve your soul*" – She was telling me that so sternly. I remember dragging my feet to church. I felt nothing. I felt empty. I wasn't even listening. I even took communion and I think the last confession I ever had was when I debated against a Franciscan monk during an Oasis of Love three-day retreat that took place in my old Architecture university retreat house. That was probably in the summer of 1999.

In 2009, I decided to diversify my program in the arts and thought I would include architecture. So, I invited my Aussie friend who used to work for the firm of Daniel Libeskind, and was working at SOM (one of the best global architecture firms) at that time to come to Cebu and do an algorithm workshop – it was more on rule-based design where their design will think for themselves based on the rules they set up. Now, we have Artificial Intelligence (AI), back then it was Rule-based design. I wasn't planning to be part of the program. I only planned to facilitate it. But the problem was the stark cultural difference. The architecture students then were quite on the GenZ stage already – wherein they were the bosses of the school. The determine their working hours and the school will adjust to them. I had to literally give them a pep talk why such a workshop was pretty important. None of my former classmates who were professors already at that time would participate. So, two, international architects working for world-famous Daniel

Libeskind, were left to just do a workshop for students instead of architect practitioners.

Because of that workshop, I established a strong rapport with the students. I eventually revived my architectural firm and a few of them became my apprentices. All of them became licensed architects a few short years after, and even founded their own firms. They were working on my father's 2nd & 3rd building. I totally was not planning to revive my architecture practice until I got a letter from the Bureau of Internal Revenue (BIR) that I have unpaid business taxes for my Design Firm that they claimed I set up since 2001. I was so shocked because I totally cannot recall setting up a business before I left for New York City, let alone a design firm! I just passed the board exam for architecture in early 2001 and on that same year, I found out that I started my own design firm. It was crazy as crazy can get. That was also the reason why I revived my firm so that I can have people to help me with the building construction since my father put me in charge of them. I didn't realize until that time how much I really loved being an architect. I am really so passionate with designing– by hand this time. I have developed a strong aversion to technology. I truly get lost making conceptual designs only to be met with resistance once I present them to my father, I became an expert on designing cheap – which is way more difficult than designing expensively. I have to innovate with local materials and experiment on my structural solutions that are not yet existing in the market. Even with my firm, I would only get one outside clients in a year at a project size of less than 300,000 pesos. It was not enough to make me survive if I had to rely on it. I was doing it out of love and of course. Beggars cannot be choosers.

My father, at that time, was resistant in making me work for him again. He still didn't get over the fact that I left him. I was the one who changed the project profile of our business who used to get an annual project sale of only 20Million pesos a year to over 200Million pesos a year. I didn't realize until I took over the family business in 2019 how painful it was for my father. It was extremely painful. Painful would be an understatement. That sounded like a lot of money but that also equates to an equal amount of liability. Our national tax agency was merciless. They waited to correct our company tax filings only 20 years after. They were notorious in doing that. Naturally, we would be liable. I will return to this later.

Because my father refused to let me work for him, I continued with my dwindling non-profit that was growing more broke. I saw an ad from Stanford looking for social entrepreneurs to join their Executive Program in Social Entrepreneurship. That was my classification back then – a "social entrepreneur." Out of over 100 applicants from across the world, I was one of those selected to be part of the Executive Program at Stanford Graduate School of Business. I only had to pay for my stay for 2 weeks. Everything else was sponsored. It was an incredible experience. The residential suites at Stanford Business School were absolutely insane. It was like a 5-star hotel with multiple meal courses offered daily from breakfast, snacks, lunch, snacks and dinner. They even included early morning exercise routine from a reputable high-end gym. I was with the Executive Director of Mayo Clinic, and other foundation from across the globe. My non-profit was literally the smallest. I was operating like the times of Medici family in Italy, where there was no structure yet that I have to work in a society counter-intuitively. I could not relate to them. They all had a structure to work with. They were all so big while mine was so — under developed, for lack of a better word. I had to rely on collaborations to survive. Nevertheless, I made excellent connections. It still didn't occur to me at this time how God has been giving me back what I have lost. In my mind, I was thinking I have a secret human benefactor making all these happen for me. I never thought of God at all. I was thinking along the lines of getting recruited by the Central Intelligence Agency (CIA). I thought, with all the people I met, the CIA must be on to me. God was totally out of the equation. God was completely none-existent in my mind all those years.

One of the benefits of my visiting artists at that time was I take them on a tour. I was so grateful to my friend, the Israeli Pianist that I paid for his scuba diving lessons. I have an old-family friend in Dumaguete City who owns an I-House like hostel and a scuba diving school was renting in one of his commercial spaces. So, I decided that we will get certified there. Since that time, I had been addicted to diving specially that my cousin from Manila was so into it too. I have always loved solo traveling. I went to Anilao in Batangas to dive in a remote island there. I will discuss in the next chapter a story of how I started clawing my way back to God. I'll start off with an introduction I wrote for my mother's book on Healing Miracles of Sr. Sto. Nino, which to this day remains my challenge with my mother. It will talk about how the highest level of demonic preternatural spirits have hi-jacked my mother.

MY MOTHER & HER HEALING CLOTH

I t is important to emphasize that as you read below, read with caution. This was written and published in **2011**. The Healing Miracles of Sto. Nino de Cebu were not confirmed to be from God. It didn't have the approval of the local bishop nor was it under investigation either. Based on the basic symptoms in spiritual warfare, how this "healing cloth" affected our lives over the years, and how it eventually evolved as more of an "anting-anting", until my mom's solemn exorcism, the miracles in this healing cloth is fundamentally from "preternatural source". I am including the narrative below because this moment in time was crucial in my return to God.

Do note that I was faking my faith the entire time I was writing this introduction. Some of the real names are withheld for confidentiality & privacy.

The Greatest Performance of Her Life –
An introduction for "The Healing Miracles
of Sto. Nino de Cebu"

For several months now, my mother has been asking me to write an introduction for her up and coming book, "Healing Miracles of Sto. Nino de Cebu". Having reminisced that, I feel quite guilty since I always find myself procrastinating. Although I have experienced the power of the healing cloth as it healed me from my monthly dose of excruciating abdominal pain every time, I get my period, the rational part of me was still skeptical. The healing cloth worked on me for the first time while I was having severe migraines. I thought I felt the heat and was able to sleep through the night. But then the next day, I was rationalizing it again and thought that I may just have psyched myself. A few months after, I had dysmenorrhea and couldn't find any pain medication tablets in my condo unit. I was desperate for relief. I recalled grabbing my mother's healing cloth, placed it on my abdomen and ranted deliriously in my prayers to God to please stop the pain forever. Since that night, I never had abdominal pains again. I couldn't forget since every time I get my period, I don't feel any pain, which is highly unusual for me. But of course, the rational part of me would constantly negotiate otherwise.

In the meantime, my mother had been worried for quite some time since she engaged Josephine "Josie" Darang, author and writer for the Philippine Daily Inquirer, to publish her book of testimonials regarding the healing cloth miracles. She was praying and asking Sr. Sto. Nino what to put on the back of her book. She felt inadequate since she never had a life and death experience unlike what was experienced by Ms. Darang, who at some point almost lost her life due to achalasia (swelling of the esophagus), but was healed through an operation, which she believed to be the biggest miracle of her life.

But on the evening of November 6, 2010, while my mother was performing with the Mother Butler Mission Guild in Laoag, Ilocos Norte for their annual dance competition, Sr. Sto. Nino immediately answered my mother's prayers. She refers to this answered prayer as the "greatest performance of her life".

What happened last November 6, 2010? While dancing to the tunes of a famous Tagalog 70s song, my mom began to labor heavily in her breathing and decided to stop before the music ended. I was told that she gracefully exited the stage without her dance mates noticing it but everyone in the back stage already noticed her groggy facial expression, her pale color, and already prepared a seat right next to stage while the ambulance was already on its way. In less than a few minutes, my mom was delivered to Laoag Memorial Hospital for quick first aid. With her was Fr. Mon and my mom's friend, Tita Malou. Both of them witnessed what happened to my mother while in the ambulance. When their doctor friend suggested to my mother to lie down and relax – even at a state of distress and pain, my mother continued to fight and refused to lie down. In her mind, "I know my body and if I lie down, I know this will be the end of my life for I will no longer be able to fight and breathe". She was coughing blood already because she couldn't breathe. Her color was turning blue. She refused to lie down because she had to continue to fight and the only way for her to fight is if she stays upright and curled up. She was already bargaining with God, with Sr. Sto Nino. In the meantime, she was already confessing to Fr. Mon, asking for forgiveness and all her last wishes. But deep down, she was embarrassed. She was begging Sr. Sto. Nino to heal her because it will be so embarrassing if she dies, knowing that her healing cloth has healed many – why can't she be healed as well? As if hearing my mother's silent plea, Fr. Mon remembered my mother's healing cloth. He found three pieces and gave it to my mother. My mom placed them on her chest.

She was immediately transferred to the Intensive Care Unit (ICU) at Don Mariano Marcos Memorial Hospital and Medical Center in Batac, Ilocos Norte, where the doctors attended to her. The initial diagnoses of the doctors were that my mom was having "pulmonary edema" or congestive heart failure and her heart was enlarged at the same time. At this stage, my mother was still conscious or she thought she was since she could sharply hear or remember hearing the diagnoses of the doctors. She continued to fight. While they were trying to put oxygen in her mouth, my mom realized that she was not getting any air. People couldn't see clearly that the mask was not on her nose but just below it due to a mix of liquid coming out of her nose and blood from her mouth. She remembered asking the nurse to please fix the oxygen mask and put it above her nose so she can breathe.

While at the ICU, all her group at Mother Butlers Mission Guild was praying over her. They were very concerned and my mother kept on saying sorry for not having finished the dance and she felt sorry that they didn't win. Fortunately, even though my mother exited the stage sooner, nobody in the audience noticed it, not even Imelda Marcos. On this note, her group told her that they won the first prize and that Imelda Marcos even gave an additional 100,000 pesos for their group. This truly made my mother happy and filled with pride, but also felt a bit of regret that she didn't hang around long enough to have a photo with Imelda Marcos.

Yes, this is my mother. Even in the midst of danger, she still found a way to find humor or something to laugh about. She was literally almost flat-lined, out of air in the Intensive Care Unit (ICU), and she still managed to think about having a photo with "the very beautiful, Imelda Marcos" as per her description.

It is important to note that it wasn't so long ago, from October 14-26th, 2010, that my mother went on a pilgrimage tour in the Holy Land with Fr. Mon along with other 33 travelers from Cebu. She climbed the 750 steps (up and down, approximately 7 kilometers each way) in Mt. Sinai, walked several kilometers in Israel and Jordan, and as soon as she arrived in Cebu, she proceeded to her highly aerobic dance rehearsals every single night for the whole week prior to November 6. On November 5th, she called my dad and reported to him that she already has difficulty breathing. My father sternly warned her to not overwork herself, and reminded her that she is no longer young so she must not overstress her heart. My mother promised that she would behave.

However, on the day itself, she saw Imelda Marcos. She wanted to come close to Imelda early that night to get a photo with her but she was called in for final rehearsal. Right after the rehearsal was already the dance number. Her breathing was already labored although her blood pressure showed that she only had 130/90, which was considered normal. In her mind, she really wanted her group to win first prize like always so that Imelda Marcos will give the award. She already pictured their group winning and she would be in front, next to Imelda Marcos. Now we know, it didn't end that way.

I was in Batangas that night when I suddenly got a call from Fr. Mon around 11 PM, informing me that my mother was in the ICU. I just finished with my 3 dives that day, and was very tired that I could have easily dosed off – dead asleep. Fortunately, I couldn't sleep that night because I had problems breathing. During my night dive (approximately 7 PM), I had breathed dry air and must have hurt my esophagus. All throughout dinner until very late in the evening, I have been having problems breathing, felt piercing pain from my chest every time I swallow and breath (coincidentally, about the same time my mother was having difficulty breathing as well). When I got the call, I found myself sitting on the floor, shaking in shock and fear from what I just heard. I was advised by Fr. Mon that I can get a bus from Manila to Batac. At that point, I was in an island called "Anilao". I called my dive master, Johnny, and told him about my mother's condition. He was so compassionate and asked the resort owner if they could find me a vehicle that would drive me to Manila. Fortunately, we did! God is so good! It was a foggy evening in Batangas and the driver could barely see anything on the road due to the fog but it was as if an angel guarded us. The road was clear and the drive was pretty smooth. When I reached Patras Bus Terminal, I was told that the earliest trip to Batac won't leave until 5:30 am. I called my brother in Manila, who was planning to take the Tuguegarao flight to get to Batac to drive with me instead. He was not familiar with the road so he asked me to look for a driver who can drive to Batac. I just asked anyone on the terminal. Out of the blue, a taxi driver from Abra (town next to Ilocos Norte) offered to drive us for 6,000 pesos. We immediately accepted because we felt we were running out of time. We reached Batac at approximately 1PM on the 7th.

When I got there, I never saw my mom so weak and exhausted. She was already breathing fine, no more oxygen mask but all the wires (ECG, etc) were still attached to her body. Her vital signs seemed to look pretty stable. In the ICU were three of my mother's mother butler friends, Tita Carmen, Tita Pilar, and Tita Lily. Next to them was my mom's volunteer helper, Saning. Next to my mother's bed is another ICU patient, whose ECG machine keeps on going off due to very unstable heart rate, yet my mom continued to sleep peacefully. She would wake up from time to time to look for me, but she would go back to sleep right after. Later in the evening, my mom was back to her good old jolly mood. She was already complaining playfully that her food taste kind of bland. Her diet of course was strictly low salt, low fat.

The next day, she was becoming extremely restless. She was talking to Saning endlessly, and she had talked to the caretaker on the next bed about her healing cloth and asked them to put it on where it caused pain to the patient next to her. Right after lunch, we were moved to the 5th floor of the main building. Dr. Lando, brother of Tita Lily has arranged everything. I would like to specially thank his and his family's wholehearted support and generosity all throughout this ordeal. Their support has truly been instrumental in keeping my mom safe and well while in Batac. There are not enough words to thank them for their kindness. There were no vacant private rooms in the hospital but he was able to arrange the director's room to be my mother's private room. It was a big, beautiful spacious room with private bath and a small sala next to the bedroom. We stayed in that room until November 10th. During the entire time, my mom was talking to all the nurses and guests that came to check on her, telling them about her experience and her healing cloth, and how their group won the dance competition even if she didn't finish. They were all looking forward to Sr. Sto. Nino and the healing cloth. She even got herself invited again to Batac, to speak about her experience and she specially requested that Imelda Marcos would also be there so she can finally get her photo with her. On the morning of November 9th, my mother was informed that the patient right next to her was finally able to urinate (even if his kidneys were already severely damaged). He felt relieved. We were told that the doctors already gave up on him. The following day, we were told that the patient already passed away but he went off smoothly. He wasn't in pain when he died. Their caretakers were thanking my mom for the healing cloth because it really helped eased the pain.

We checked out of the hospital late afternoon of the 10th and flew back to Manila. We immediately checked in to St. Luke Hospital at Global City, Fort Bonifacio for further tests. Based on the X-Ray and 2D Echo results, it was further diagnosed that my mom only had about 42% ejection/contraction of her heart. While in Batac, it was also seen on X-ray results that my mother had an enlarged heart. On this note, a doctor of St. Luke's recommended for an angiogram and considered the possibility of an angioplasty.

My mother, however, panicked. So did my dad and they insisted they return to Cebu and if the procedure was really necessary, they'd rather do it in Cebu. We left St. Luke hastily the following day.

On November 12th, we met with a cardiologist to consult her about my mom's case. Based on the doctors' diagnosis from both Mariano Marcos Hospital and St. Luke's, she supported the angiogram recommendation of the doctor from St. Luke. She suggested my mom pray for discernment. On that same day, my mom held a thanksgiving mass in our building lead by Fr. Mon, along with her prayer group in Brotherhood of Christian Businessmen and Professionals (BCBP) and mother butler. They all prayed for discernment and my mother decided (with my father's consent) that they would go for the angiogram. Praise God! That same night, I sent a text to the cardiologist. She suggested we checked in the following day so she could do her angiogram by Monday but my mom still wanted to watch the Pacquiao fight Sunday morning so we pushed it for Sunday evening. Immediately upon check in, another round of blood tests began. My mom brought many Sto. Nino's with her this time and she started giving them to the nurses, cleaning people, etc. She would talk about her near-death experience and the healing cloth. At first, as usual, there was still hesitation from the recipients. After some time, more and more people where coming in.

The first doctor that mom met as soon as she was admitted to Cebu Doctor's University (CDU) Hospital, told us that she knew of a patient that has been unconscious (asleep) for quite some time, blood pressure or heart rate was very slow and kept on slowing down. They were all expecting that he would probably die pretty soon. My mom and I suggested to just try put the cloth on him. It's very hard for me to continue rationalizing since I was completely in the middle of everything. I saw many direct testimonials and I seriously experienced many unexplainable scenarios. She was afraid that he would wake up and if he does, she would be very scared. We continued to urge her that there's really no harm —it's worth a try. We didn't expect that she would really do it. She just wiped the cloth on the arm of the patient. The next day, the nurse informed her that her patient opened his eyes. Curious, she went up to check him out. At first, she thought it was just a seizure since the patient was staring right at her, his eyes were not blinking and not moving. Then suddenly, his left hand grasp her hand and she thought – this must be a seizure. She plied her hand out of the grasp and suddenly, the patient's other hand held her recently released hand. Then she was convinced that the patient was really awake. They put the patient back on oxygen after that. Since it can't be explained rationally, it is not quite believable that the doctor will connect it with her wiping the patient with the healing cloth. But what are the odds? With just a wipe of the cloth, the patient whom they considered to be dying and had been asleep for a long time suddenly wakes up?

The next day, the doctor presented my mom's condition to her fellow doctors as an "interesting case". Based on the reports from St. Luke, it showed that her heart was enlarged and that the functionality of her heart was very bad. However, based on recent x-ray done in CDU, there were no traces of enlargement. I could still remember what the doctors' in Batac said about my mom's heart, "ang laki nang heart ni tita, abot pati sa right chest [Tita has a very big heart, it reached the right chest].

Many of the doctors came to visit her to ask for further verification of her story. On Wednesday morning, she had her angiogram and the results were very good. The cardiologist told me that there was very minimal blockage on one artery only, not significant enough to require angioplasty, not significant enough to cause edema or attack. They still don't know what caused the Pulmonary Edema but they do not see any cardiac connection. Praise God!

Over the days, my mom's room was always filled with people. Our stock of St. Nino, continue to run out. We had to constantly ask our helper to deliver new sets, until later, my mother had to bring all her key ingredients in; (1) Sto. Nino statues (over 100 pcs), (2) healing cloths and original blouse worn when my mother released her oil, (3) plastic containers and ribbons. My mom's bed didn't look like a hospital bed. The room looked like a production area of Sr. Sto. Nino. It looked like a store, except; my mom was giving away Sto. Nino statues with her labor of love folded paper bases. Knocks on the door didn't stop even until the day we left. New text messages came about that more miracles had happened. I hope you will be inspired on the testimonials of more healing miracles of Sto. Nino de Cebu on the following pages of this book. According to my mother, Sto. Nino is like a child that cares for all living things. You will find on the following pages that miracles don't only work on people but also on cats, dogs, pigs, birds, and on every living thing.

❦

So, what's wrong with the Healing Cloth?

For more than 10 years, my mother and I have been distributing this healing cloth in over 20 countries we have traveled to across the world. We would go on a group tour and pilgrimage every year all throughout Central Europe, Turkey, Africa, and so many more.

But when did I realize there was something wrong with my mom's healing cloth? It was when my mom would start healing by herself by touching the patient. I felt an ickiness about that and so did my dad. He would tell her to stop it as it might have a different side effect on her. She would use the healing cloth in the slot machine, hoping that it will bring her luck. I had that natural distaste each time she does that. Even back then, I feel really icky each time I go inside a Casino. I feel a darkness all around me – even when I was still faithless. I never felt comfortable each time I'm in one.

Later, there used to be the image of Sr. Sto. Nino when she gives out the healing cloth. We would hear of people telling my mom it's demonic, and in defense of my mom, I would get angry. Most of the people that would criticize her were Protestants or born-again Christians, so all the more they weren't able to convince me because they had a reputation to be sacrilegious when it came to dealing with religious images.

But overtime, I noticed, my mom was just giving away the cloth, without the Sto. Nino image anymore. It is important to note that I got my faith back during the pilgrimage going to the Vatican to attend the Canoninization of St. Pedro Calungsod. It was also the time my youngest nephew Marco died, just a week before the trip. I was already faking my faith since this time – when my mom first got her oil flowing from her ribs back in 2009. My mom came home and said there was oil in her body. My mom's friend started believing it must have healing properties. Shortly after that, the word spread out. People started coming to our building to touch my mom. I felt very uncomfortable and embarrassed. I was worried that people will be lining up in our building because of this. It's exactly what happened. She would give the cloth to everyone and I will just cover my face. Up until the Batac incident, I remained resistant to my mom's healing cloth.

So how do we know if a miracle or an unnatural event is a supernatural one? When we say supernatural, it refers to God, and God alone. We have to know that not all goodness belongs to God because demons love to deceive people by imitating what feels good, what looks good and what people usually perceive as "good" such as healing. There is another kind of power that doesn't belong to God, and these are preternatural powers. Do remember that from the book of **Genesis 1:1-3**, God created the heavens on the second (2nd) day – this was the time when the angels who disobeyed were cast to hell and those who abstained were cast to earth, which also means the same as hell, eventually. But in spite of this, God never removed their heavenly powers – to which in their case are no longer heavenly, but are preternatural. Occultists, warlords, or people or practice witchcraft get their powers from a preternatural source – otherwise called *demons*. When demons oppress a person thru a hex, some people get sick and since it is a spiritual sickness, often times, there aren't any diagnosis. It will remain a medical mystery. That's what happened to my mom and everybody else who got a reaction or sort of healing from the "healing cloth" – but were they really healed? The answer is no. Because my mom, at that time she released her oil was not in a state of grace. So why will demons heal if they are evil? Of course, their objective is to divert people's trust in the Lord away from God. Their objective is to let people focus on beliefs that has nothing to do with Jesus and will willfully disobey the authority of the Roman Catholic Church.

When did I start with Spiritual Warfare?

In 2012, while on the bus to the Vatican, I met someone who was a member of the charismatic ministry called, *Bukas Loob sa Dios (BLD)*. She shared with us her spiritual journey and as I was listening to her talk about a friend of hers who used to have a lot of sexual partners, she explained that one day, that woman approached a priest because she grew tired of her life, and that she wanted to settle down. Her spiritual director told her about soul ties. That was when I first learned about soul ties. Her spiritual director gave her a prayer to break soul ties that she had to pray for at least six months. And true enough, after six months, she met someone who eventually became her husband. They got married in the Roman Catholic Church. She then proceeded to sharing her story about her brother who got possessed. Again, I was so fascinated. I should be scared but instead, I was fascinated. This was also the moment where I just suddenly had the awareness that I had faith. The feeling was akin to someone who had *amnesia* but then suddenly, they got their memory back. That's how it was like for me. I felt like I had been out in the cold - naked for so long, and suddenly, I have been cloaked in the protective warmth of God's embrace. I knew then I never want to be without God, ever again.

After the pilgrimage, I was decided already to be involved in spiritual warfare. Since I didn't really have any community to ask from yet at that time, I was doing it all on my own. I googled "exorcism" and followed Fr. Lampert. I watched exorcism horror movies. For some reason, I was very driven to fight demons. I was so obsessed that I compiled a two-hour long deliverance prayers following a specific sequence. The sequence was correct – the prayer was extremely powerful, which involved "rebuking" of spirits, which, if I had known any better, I should have prayed only inside the Blessed Sacrament. Though I confessed before I started, it wasn't a proper confession. It means, there were still so many mortal sins I have committed that I wasn't aware of yet at that time. I also made an army of my little nieces who were really broken children because their father, who is my 2nd elder brother, separated with their mother.

At that time, I was more their parents because my brother was in Manila and he was too angry with his ex-wife that he couldn't think of his kids yet at that time. I took care of them. In my own way, I loved those kids. They were difficult kids – because they were as broken as me so sometimes, I could not control myself when the eldest would talk back at me. I would end up hitting her. The eldest was literally the most bitter of them all, but she can be quite scared with the idea of me hitting her so she was a little easier to manage. She would also be quite cruel with her own siblings and she would hit them too. I was at my worst with the middle child, who was the kindest of them all but she can be quite obstinate among them. She was never violent but has our temper and when she says no to something, no matter what, nobody can make her do anything, even if it gets her beat. That was how firm she tends to get – she was more like me, except that, she was so much kinder than me. But back then, we were tight. I know that I really cared for them more than anyone in my family who eventually benefited from all the hard work I did for these kids. I was helping them process their emotions, in the same way I was also processing mine. We were always together and I was content not having anyone. I was content being single because I had them and my eight dogs in my condo. My nieces were staying with my parents but I would ask them to stay with me in the condo every once in a while, but almost every day, we go out together.

All of them started out hating their father. At that time, I was quite loyal to my brother back then and it would irritate me a lot when they would talk bad about my brother being an irresponsible father. I would defend my brother to them and I would emphasize that they should be thankful that he got them instead of staying with their mother side. They were looking at their mother side with rose-colored lenses. Regardless, they were my prayer warriors. We were all broken, bitter and angry. We would complain the following day, of being beaten up in our sleep. We were fearless since we were pretty much angry with everything about the world. The concept of being afraid of any demons were inconsequential to us. I, personally, prayed non-stop almost daily, for two hours each time at home, in hotels, in ships, in cars, when we travel abroad and so many more for seven straight years.

I was relentless. I had zero concept of retaliation because I have been so used to all my suffering at that time that I really had no concept of peace. I just took pleasure in the thought I was beating up the demons with my prayers. I didn't have any concept of transforming as well. I was still angry as angry can get. My helpers would leave me all the time. I would have conflicts even with my father's workers who were my cousins from my mother side. And I used to have an office in my mother's building but because I have a really poor reputation at home, worsened by my mother's negative stories, they always end up leaving me because my mother and their helpers would constantly tell them how awful I am. My mother is a very likeable person and when it is my own mother ruining my reputation, people would always believe. I am no match at all. Except that at that time, I always had my father – who would always support me. It would aggravate my mom's irritation against me.

I remember always begging my mom to love me and I would ask her, "Do you love me mommy?" and my mom would honestly say to me curtly, "I'm sorry! No matter how hard I try, I just don't love you! I don't know why but I don't love you!". Remembering this, still bring tears in my eyes. This is a sign that I have not yet healed from this memory. For as long as it can still make me cry, it will always remain an open door for me. In a way, I understand now, why I feel so compelled to write my story. God is making me process all my open doors as what I have been doing to our patients. There is truly no shortcut to healing. None. We have to go thru the most horrible memories and forgive those memories. Until we forgive those, we won't ever be free.

My mom is truly a very good person. She is a very forgiving person. She literally forgives everyone who hurt her and mind you, these people really hurt my mom in ways that most people will find unforgivable. My mom even forgave my father's mistresses. My mom even forgave my father, even more. And her forgiveness was truly what lead to my father's conversion. That is how golden her heart is. Even I, cannot dispute it. But there is really one person that my mother just cannot forgive and love, no matter how hard she tries — herself, and I became her collateral damage. I understand completely why. I understand my mother completely and the reason why she cannot love me. In a nutshell, it had nothing to do with me.

Before I narrate the reason why I understand where my mother is coming from and why she hated me so much, let me share with you how I grew to love my mother and how I started seeing her differently that I could not hate her anymore. I started understanding why. And this was also how I realized why her healing cloth cannot be from God because at the time she got it, she was not in a state of grace precisely because of this reason. How did I know she was not in a state of grace? Because she has something deep within her that she continually refused to acknowledge and give up until today that is preventing her complete spiritual healing. I'll walk you thru my years of purification, from 2018 up until 2022, the year my mother almost died in Miller Hospital in another chapter.

I learned from my dad's cousin that my mom told her why she tried to abort me — because she initially only wanted three children. I would assume, maybe because she didn't want the number "4", which is not a good number in their "Chinese-Buddhist" belief system.

Another is, my mom survived all the trauma, struggle, pain, betrayal and so many negative events that happened to her by her choosing to change the story. She was able to survive because she will not entertain the truth, which was negative but fabricate a new story that was positive. It's almost like using a pathological lie as a force for good. The question is, is that okay?

If we go back to the time when Rebecca asked Jacob to deceive Isaac into giving him his birthright that he wanted to give to Essau, God permitted it because she was fulfilling God's objective will. Even so, Jacob had to pay for it tremendously all throughout his lifetime (*Genesis 27:1-30*). Perhaps, am I supposed to pay for my mom's trespasses too, throughout my lifetime, as Jacob did in order to cut the curse of disobedience and dishonesty? That would make sense, right?

In fact, at the height of my hatred and anguish towards my mom, what comforted me was the fact that I have Mama Mary as my mother. As I kept on praying to Mama Mary – I noticed that my feelings towards my mom had gradually changed. I no longer hated her. I began to understand her. Until I learned to love her again.

That is the power of suffering. If I were to do it all over again, I would always choose to be the sacrificial lamb, because that would mean, the power to transform our reality is within my reach. When my mom and dad had their problems, I wanted to believe they will get better. I kept the hope that they will be okay. I didn't used to have a sweet relationship with my father until I watched the movie, "Clueless" and when I saw how the daughter regarded her dad, I decided, I will do the same for my dad. Over the years, my dad learned to appreciate it that it became normal for us eventually.

Being a victim soul – if we do it faithfully, and authentically, has the significant power to transform the hardest hearts, my own included.

REJECTING DIVORCE

My father had a 30-year relationship with his mistress. I was 10 years old when I found out my dad was cheating with my mom's secretary. This secretary was a young lady my mom saw walking on the streets, bleeding because her feet got stabbed by a banana-cue stick. She took her in, fed her, put her to school – to college too, and made her their secretary that they both share with my dad. The next thing I knew, our family was falling apart.

My father chose an apartment right across the school of my brothers. One day, my brothers, along with their classmates saw my father moving in with our secretary. One can just imagine how my brothers felt at that time. They didn't say anything to my mom. My dad would always come home bringing us ice cream every night. My sister and I would enjoy it. Until one day, my mom finally found out. I thought they will separate. My father was a very intelligent man but can be quite abusive too – he could manipulate us to accept him and his conditions.

But there was something so remarkable with my father despite him being physically, emotionally and mentally abusive at times— we all know my father have the "purest" heart ever. He is a very good man. Even though he used to beat us when he got irritated with all the mental stresses he was going through; even though he had another woman, my father was always a very good provider, not just money wise but parental guidance wise. My father always went over and beyond to provide for us. He would drive us to school every day and he was our walking encyclopedia. But he was very tough with my brothers. He would beat them unless they obeyed him. And they did especially in his choice of college courses for them.

I remember my father, apologizing to me and my sister, that he was much too "weak" to leave us. And I remember my sister telling my dad, *"That doesn't make you weak for not having the courage to leave us dad- that makes you strong."* I remembered my dad looking stricken. I remembered going to their apartment and when the mistress was talking back to my mom, I was so angry that I grabbed her by the hair and she fell off the bed. I was only 10 years old but I was really quite strong. My dad beat me after that.

We had a family meeting where my father was very upfront with all of us. He said, that he will wait until I finish college before he and my mother will officially separate. My mom handled it very well. Although there was a time, my mom almost drove her car off the bridge but because she didn't want us to have a broken family, she decided to take whatever my father was offering.

My mom talked to each one of us, asking us to help her love our dad so that he won't be pushed to leave us because he will feel that he doesn't feel loved anymore. They still shared the same office with my dad. My mom truly was just playing it cool. She would be the talk of the town of our neighbors – people would call her martyr but she maintained a happy face, while deep down, she was already hurting very badly. Every night, my father would go home to their apartment with his mistress and during the day, he goes to work with my mom – where they remained cordial with each other. It remained like that over the years. Until I graduated college, and became an Architect.

I forgot about their deal with my mom by the time I graduated college because my father seemed to have grown obsessed with my mom. They always go out on a date during the day – they were very sweet, just like lovers. But at night, my father would go back to their apartment. It was almost like my mom was the mistress, and the mistress was the wife. It went on like that for another 15 years or so. I recall my father getting hospitalized and my mother was out of the country, this was in 2008 – the time where my mother had to move to Manila to be with my 2nd elder brother because his wife left him for another man. His business was falling apart because his ex-wife tried to ruin him among his clients. She blamed him for losing her great love, who happened to be a married man also. My brother always had this uncanny way of getting back at his wife or at anyone, where it will really hurt, although I think he was also trying to save his marriage and the other guy's marriage, as well. But his ex-wife was much too broken for repair at that time. They were actually two of a kind – he had met his match.

She was quite a dangerous woman to mess with. It's like "hell hath no fury with a woman scorned".

While in the hospital, the mistress came to my dad's hospital room. They were talking endearingly to each other and I just pretended to sleep. I was so hurt. I loved my father so much but I felt so betrayed. It was my mom he was betraying but I still felt so betrayed.

Since I was praying the *Healing of the Family Tree*, *Breaking of Soul Ties* and *Breaking of Generational Curses* for seven years, I noticed my father growing more and more clingy towards my mom. He would get jealous when a widower we traveled with on a pilgrimage in Europe would send my mom a box of frozen fish – those were pretty innocent gifts but I remember my mom telling me to be quiet about it because the last time she mentioned it to my dad, he got very jealous and told her never to accept any more gifts again. They were already in their 60's.

Later, my dad would comment on my FB page defending *divorce*– that's when I had it. I messaged my dad to please stop commenting on my wall about defending divorce because people might figure out the reason why I am still single is because of him. My father apologized. I don't know how it impacted my father because since that chat, things have been changing with him. As his Parkinson's disease progressed, and he started forgetting things, he grew clingier to my mother.

My dad would spend on all of my mom's desires; From new cars, to traveling abroad, to investing in my mom's direct selling business, to her slot machine addiction, to jewelries, to lavish birthday parties, and to a super grand *golden wedding*, while my father refused to buy himself a brand-new car, refused to let us buy him expensive pairs of shoes. One time, my mom, sister and I, tried to trick my dad into accepting a high-quality leather pair of shoes from us. We told the sales lady to switch the pricing of a very cheap pair of shoes to their most expensive ones.

When we asked our dad to try it on, he refused to believe the price. Mind you, we were paying, not him. But he stood up, went snooping on the display and found out the price of the shoes we were buying him. He got so mad and demanded we leave. He didn't even buy the cheap pair of shoes. My father was never materialistic but he would always give us very expensive gifts, except himself. My father is absolutely the most generous man I have ever known. My mom is very generous too but nothing compares to my dad. My dad would drive around the city listening to a radio station, waiting for someone asking or needing help. He would ask my mom to give help provided that she will not disclose it's coming from him. For as long as I can remember, my father would do that almost every night.

About my father, he used to work in Manila at the National Power Corporation (NPC). He was one of the very few Electricians at that time selected as they only accept the very best. Actually, at that time, only two of them were selected from Cebu. After NPC, he decided to start his own merchandising business in Cebu with all his life savings. But as luck would have it – he was duped by his landlord after paying everything, all his merchandise were completely lost when the landlord took everything; contracts were not a common practice in the 70s. The landlord padlocked everything and he was left with a suitcase as the only furniture he and my mom had in a windowless room.

Desperate and hungry, with three children (at that time, I wasn't born yet), he decided to pawn his most prized possession at that time, his soldering gun. The money he got he used as fare to repair typewriters in Colon, enough to earn him his start-up capital, once again. He went to a bookstore – just looking for ideas how to earn money. He happened to be a genius with a photographic memory. He saw a book about fire protection. Read it from cover to cover in one seating.

My dad was a genius. He had two degrees in USC, electrical and mechanical engineering. He taught part time in Cebu Central College (currently called University of Cebu), where he found an opportunity to offer the college owner, a win-win deal – he will install his fire sprinkler system in his building. He won't charge a labor fee until the system worked. After that the rest was history. Our family business was already more than 40 years old, and it all started with a book he read in a bookstore. Of course, he attended several fire protection training and seminars after that, and equipped himself with the best fire protection literature from around the world when he could afford it.

My dad pretty much invented and innovated, most of our systems. It's just too bad he didn't really have the institutional support at that time, and with a family in tow, and more families from his workers, majority of his life was in the service of his workers and clients. My mom would tell me that when they used to live in Manila, my dad would always make it a point he will go home to her and my brother.

There was even a time that he almost fell riding in the jeepney that was so full because he lacked sleep.

My father always loved my mother. My father was just a victim of his own father too. During the burial of my grandmother's youngest sister, I met with a few relatives who knew about my grandmother. I learned that my grandmother was widowed young. She married an army man, and she was so in love with him. They had one child, my late Aunt Nelida or we would call her, Tita Nelly. But her husband died in the war. Back in the day, during those times, since my grandmother was widowed young, her parents were still looking for a husband for her. Here came my grandfather who happened to be a teacher.

My grandfather was also a genius so he easily won the approval of my great grandparents. My grandmother didn't want to get married again but she had no choice. So, on their wedding night, I learned that she was raped by my grandfather. It was marital rape and my father was conceived that night. Imagine, how it affected my father and he knew about it too as he grew older. My grandmother though, loved my father so much. It didn't matter that my grandmother loved him so much, but the primal wound caused by my grandfather was already etched in my father's DNA. My father used to be a seminarian. He studied in Don Bosco, a Salesian, in Victorias City, Negros Occidental. Somewhere along the way, he lost his faith – because of misplaced shame.

He once shared with me the story when he lost a watch lent to him by his father. He was so scared. He was in the middle of the sugar cane farm, kneeling and praying to Mama Mary, begging her to help him find the watch. Lo and behold, he found it. He narrated how he felt absolute shame for begging Mama Mary over something so trivial. In his shame, he stopped praying to Mama Mary and vowed he never will in order to not bother her. His intention meant well but I surmised, his shame was the reason why he lost his faith. Shame is pride. We have to be careful with shame. Our incapacity to be humble is what causes shame. Persecution of the self, which is something God, in his infinite mercy for us, will never do to us for as long as we are humble enough to recognize our weaknesses. Shame grows when we refuse to believe in God's mercy.

My father always wished that old people should have access to an institutional support on how to get old and deal with memory loss due to old age; and this should be available in our society. It was painful to see my father, who used to have a photographic memory, fall into depression when he suffered these early signs of dementia. Denial is a problem.

I remember my dad always telling me, *"This should be taught in school earlier on - on how to manage life and aging, and how to prepare for it..."* He never thought this would happen to him and he could already see it happening. I felt extremely powerless to help him then.

I love my dad. He is still alive and he is getting way better, mood and cognition-wise, thank God! But had these services been available earlier on with a more approachable, alert, observant and less academic social support system in our healthcare system, the degenerative effects of dementia could very well be prevented, reduced and managed early on. Though I remain thankful to God for this miracle but I know, it could have been less painful for him and all of us, if such kind of institutional support and information dissemination of this particular illness is made accessible to everyone earlier on.

I hope our government, at any stage or level, would realize there are so many more institutional support systems needed for our people from birth to include, old age. There are so many more noteworthy projects to establish far more worth it, than the acquisition of more money – such as quality of life (mental, emotional and psychological) that money cannot really buy; especially when one is hit with an illness like this as one ages. Money cannot bring back lost memories and cognition.

I always wished that someday, I could take my dad to the best libraries in the world. The most that I managed to do was buy him his first IPAD, which he never would have bought for himself, that gave him access to pretty much all information he wanted at his heart's content. Physically, I managed to tour him around New York city and to the Getty Museum in Los Angeles, before his dementia/ Alzheimer's had progressed.

There is another detail I haven't mentioned yet, and that I have a younger half-brother. He is two (2) years younger than me. The mother was also my parent's former secretary. When my father found out she was pregnant, my father started looking for a good husband for her. And my dad asked my mom to help him. The dating sites at that time was via snail mail – *Pen Pals*. My mom and dad carefully selected her future husband. And they picked out a very good German man who had a very good business in Germany. He was an excellent husband and an excellent father to my half-brother.

He even asked my father to let my brother use his last name, to which my father agreed and willfully signed off.

I met my younger brother when he was just a toddler. But, when he turned 15, he came to the Philippines with his mother. His mother asked help from my mom because my brother finally realized that he wasn't his father's son. He realized he looked so different from his siblings. He asked his mother why he doesn't look like them. So, his mother explained the situation. My brother was so disappointed and chastised his mother for sleeping with a married man. What was incredibly amazing was that, it was my mom who picked up my half-brother in the airport, with his mother on the front seat. It was my mother comforting my half-brother to understand and to learn to appreciate the fact that he now has two families that care for him. My mother was touring them around. During this time, my father went into hiding. I called my dad because he was not around. And he told me how embarrassed he was. He kept telling me he didn't deserve my mother. He felt so ashamed of himself. My mom, ended up, wooing him to come home and show up. My father finally did. I think, it was probably that time when my father realized how much he really loved my mother.

You know what was the most remarkable thing that happened when my dad was starting to lose his memory? He pretended he didn't remember his mistress anymore. I think my father wanted to separate from his mistress for a while already but he probably felt guilty because he was, after all, the mistress' first lover. He probably felt responsible and I have no doubt he did. I knew he was pretending because he could still remember me. At the peak of my conflict with my mom, and siblings, back in 2021, I would pick up my dad to go to the lawyer so he can sign off majority of his shares to me. This was the time my mom and my brothers were making it very difficult for me to operate our business. He would still remind me to make sure that all the documents didn't have loop holes and he would remind me to review it, again and again. We had to revise the documents more than twice. And in those occasion, my father's mistress was our witness. So, if he knew her to be a witness, and calls her by her first name, but when it came down to going home and the mistress asked him if he would prefer to stay in his apartment, my father would then ask her, *"who are you again?"* I witnessed that for myself.

My only other support at that time was my father's mistress. What are the odds of that happening before? Zero.

When my father's dementia initially started, my father was very violent. Very angry. He refused to sleep. He would always drive as far as he could. My mom grew tired of accompanying him at very late hours. We couldn't find a caregiver that could handle my dad at that time. So, my mom, being always wise as she is, called my father's mistress. My dad's mistress, over the years, have grown to respect my mom's authority again. So, when my mom called her and instructed her to keep my dad company, she agreed. It is important to note that the mistress was just recovering from cancer so accompanying my dad in the wee hours of the morning really took a toll on her.

Until one time, my father was arrested in Badian, about two hour drive from the city. He hit a tricycle and tried to lose them. They later caught up with him and arrested him. Thank God, nobody was injured. No charges were filed.

That early morning, my dad left without the mistress. He just decided to drive on his own. We were so worried. My father's mistress called my mom because he was suddenly gone. We called my aunt from Davao who managed to find out from her connections in the military that my father was arrested. My father was also a victim of extortion. There was someone who would keep on sending text messages to my father who claimed he was with the New People's Army (NPA) and somehow there were these veiled threats against us. My father has always been putting all of our safety first. There were so many things we didn't know of but my father was always protecting us. Since that time, we didn't allow our dad to drive anymore. My brothers insisted for dad to stay with my mom since that time.

But God is good all the time, and all the time, God is good. I would not have the opportunity to learn about my mom and my dad's history if divorce was available when I was 10 years old. My half-brother would have not reconciled with his mother, had my mom and dad divorced because my mother wouldn't have been around to comfort him. There wouldn't have been a golden wedding to speak of if they divorced. I wouldn't have the opportunity to experience this remarkable life and conversion if they divorced. I wouldn't be writing this memoir if my parent's divorced.

What people always need is time. Time to accept. Time to forgive. Time to heal. And most importantly, time to recover. I learned the hard way that the only way for a person to heal from our trauma is to face the trauma head on. How to do that? It's not avoidance but acceptance. To overcome abuse is to grow more confident in God's love that no amount of criticism can make one question one's sense of self. Confidence cannot be acquired by justification. Confidence is acquired thru endurance. *ENDURANCE* is the buzzword.

Many talk about divorce because their husbands are abusive. That's why they believe divorce is the answer. Even if one divorce one's spouse, the trauma caused will still follow wherever one goes. The trauma, which caused one's self-pity will still follow us around and infect other people with it. Until a person has healed, that brokenness will still follow that person around.

It is a mistake for a person to think that when a person files for divorce, one is free. Instead, they accomplished the opposite. They didn't deal with the abuse because they didn't change the manner they reacted to the abuse. They didn't deal with the abuse because they didn't change the way they reacted to prevent the abuse. They didn't deal with the abuse because they ran away from it.

God allows separation. God even allows annulment (which is subject to his permission and in his perfect time). Annulment is even better because it makes the marriage null & void if it's fundamentally invalid to begin with. Divorce can never ever be better than Annulment. Annulment is more than sufficient.

Though God allows separation and annulment, God does not allow adultery. If one needs to be separated from one's abuser until one has recovered, then do so. Give oneself time. Time to heal before one tries one's hand at freedom again. Some wounds take a lifetime to heal so jumping from one relationship to another will definitely not make anyone heal.

God is truly the best healer even if to heal means one has to overcome a horrific act by allowing one to be subjected to more of those. What God wants us to learn is how we alter the way we react to an abusive situation. We alter the way we respond to an abusive situation. Not just what others see but how we see ourselves. Until we grow more confident with our love for God, we can never respond to an abusive situation in a way that heals us.

This is where the virtue of suffering comes in. Suffering is a virtue. Because when we love – truly love, we suffer. The measure of how much we truly love is based on our capacity to suffer.

When couples get married under God, they do so because they are supposed to love God above all. More than each other. Because if they love God More, they will be willing to suffer for their spouse because nothing can be greater than their love for their creator.

There is no one greater than our creator. God should be our benchmark for love.

In a recent event, God had demonstrated to me, that I still don't love God enough the way that God loves me because I got affected by other people's opinion of me. I didn't have the confidence of God's love because I allowed myself to feel self-pity. When we allow that, we give the spirit of rage, hate and retaliation the opportunity to penetrate our soul. I realized that if I truly loved God with all of my heart, I wouldn't have retaliated even if I felt justified. I was demanding exactly that. Justice. That is the same demand battered or abused wives are demanding. Justice – that's why they want divorce.

But take a look at St. Monica. How did she respond to abuse? She responded thru silent prayer, sacrifice and increased love. More love. What justice did she acquire? Her silent endurance and love have led to the conversion of her spouse & son, St. Augustine. It took St. Monica an entire lifetime of suffering to bear those fruits. And with that fruit, his son was able to convert more people generations after that. Even until today.

As for me, I failed. Miserably. In most of my challenges as an adult. Though I didn't retaliate at the heights of my pain, I retaliated each time my pain subsided because it's often replaced with rage and anger. In my recent conflict where I felt I was bullied, yet again, God gave me the grace to suffer immediately because if he left me on my own, God knows I won't be able to survive it. God knows I won't be able to come back to him. Suffering is a grace.

When one is suffering, God is even so much closer to us more than ever. What one needs to watch out for is when one is no longer suffering. That's where the danger towards our soul comes in. God never let me get away with suppressing my trauma.

God let me go thru it, over and over again. Why? So, I can realize for myself that I need to love him more. I didn't realize that until God tested me. Again. With increased difficulty.

But the good thing is, I am still alive. There is still another opportunity to try again. The same goes for marriage.

Marriage under God is a sacred contract a couple made with God. Instead of supporting for a parent to divorce or couples divorcing their spouses, why don't people learn to fall in love with God first?

Focus on loving God and see if one still hates one's spouse if one has truly allowed oneself to fall in love with God. Give oneself the opportunity to love God. We have nothing to lose, just the hate and trauma.

OVERCOMING DEMONS

Suicidal

Life sucks,
Living's tough,
To live is hard,
But to breathe we must...

To die is what?
When death's unknown.
To live and die,
Why live at all?

I wrote this poem when I was in college already —
although I don't recall ever attempting to hurt myself at
the time I wrote this. It would seem it was already in my
psyche then. It was published by The International Library
of Poetry, as part of *Letters from the Soul* series under the
"Clouds Across the Stars" 2002 edition. I wrote "This poem
was written in a moment of weakness, and I believe that this
is a question often asked by many. Thus, I know that I am

not alone with this poem. This is a poem or reality expressed angry in poetry. Life is like a wheel, you don't fall off unless you stop pedaling, don't give up, and keep on living!"

I am not sure why I have a very vague memory of how I was as a Catholic before I lost my faith. I recall that my mother always let me attend *"Life in the Spirit Seminars (LSS),"* or make me join a Christian youth community. We also have annual recollection all throughout High School and first Friday masses – that whole Christian tradition. I am still confused why it didn't stick with me, while many others did. A part of me wonders if my father's infidelity and insecurity in our family was the reason why I had difficulty absorbing Christ into my heart then – although I have a vivid memory of always ranting to God for all my troubles. I was always crying and begging God to take me because I was too scared to take my own life when I was much younger.

I recall my attempt at suicide in grade school. I don't recall the reason or the trigger anymore but there was a time I tried to get a nail cutter to cut my wrist but I was much too scared to do it. I don't recall attempting again until I was already in my late 30s. I do recall I always have an **angry** communication with God. In fact, a year after Simone died, something happened to me – I forgot what made me angry but I recalled getting so angry with God that I said, "maybe the demon is the god, and you (Jesus) are the demon." I only remembered saying this only after I got my faith back in my late 30s. One can trust that God won't let us miss anything about our life and the Holy Spirit will always be there to help us look back and process our repressed memories once we surrender to him.

For as long as I can remember, I was always in pain emotionally, mentally, and psychologically. The sad thing was that – I wasted all of those pain. I spent all of those emotions without any purpose because I didn't have any concept of reparation yet. This is precisely why I am writing this book so that the young adults won't waste their pain and suffering.

After I got expelled, even if I had a very good employer already who was willing to sponsor me, enough for me to get a green card, it was no longer enough for me. I needed to be validated. Because I felt ridiculed and discriminated, I wanted to redeem my whole identity. I wasn't prepared to come home defeated with nothing to bring home. Even though I had a legitimate non-profit I can bring home to the Philippines, I decided to travel to Central Europe first before making it back home. I had an elaborate plan of starting out in London, then to a town near the Hague so I can visit an old I-House friend, then to Rotterdam, Amsterdam, Paris, Venice, Florence, Pisa, Rome, and all the way down to Naples – those were my initial itinerary before I spoke to my sister about suicide. As I was preparing my itinerary, I didn't realize, I didn't buy myself a ticket to the Philippines and I was already flying out to Europe in two weeks then. I spoke with my sister, where we talked about her neighbor who committed suicide. Her neighbor was in her 60s when she got hit by a Hummer while vacationing with her long-term boyfriend in Texas. It so happens that the state law in Texas with regards to liabilities concerning a vehicular accident that if the victim got hit because they were jaywalking, then the vehicle that hit them has zero liability. That's what happened to her. She got hospitalized for over a year. Although she didn't pay for it because she had her health insurance, her mortgage was still piling up. Just when she got out of the hospital and was finally able to return to work, there was a complication in her brain that she needed to go back to the hospital. Her insurance was already maxed out.

When she got out, she could not work anymore. To make matters worse, her boyfriend broke up with her. Her final straw was that her daughter was going to move in with her. But somehow, the daughter changed her mind. So, I told my sister, "I understand why she killed herself now. What else can she do?" then my sister said, "She could file for bankruptcy. She didn't have to kill herself". And I said, "but what's the point? She is old already." And my sister said, "so what? At least she is still alive. There is always something she can do." And for some reason, I didn't realize I was thinking aloud when I said "it's true, she is 60 and she can still do something. How much more me? I'm not even in my 30's yet." Then my sister snapped at me and said, "What? Why? Are you thinking of killing yourself?!" That really jolted me. Until my sister asked me that, I wasn't aware that I was already thinking of killing myself. That was in 2007.

Just to give a short anecdote while I was a Resident Fellow at I-House. The first time I applied for a resident fellow position, our final interview involved role playing. The counselor was a very good actor and when she role played the role of the suicidal resident, I actually felt very scared. I panicked because it was so realistic. Talking about God was also taboo when dealing with suicidal patients and what she needed to hear me say was, "are you thinking of killing yourself?" I needed to ask her that question.

So up until I was asked by my sister, I didn't realize how crucial it was. That's the only time I truly appreciated the question. I understood then that a seriously suicidal person is detached from oneself. God saved me then because that conversation wasn't planned yet it happened out of nowhere. That was the time I realized that I was planning to kill myself in Naples. Even the hotel I chose in Naples was so dingy that if I didn't awaken from my suicidal hypnotism, I might have killed myself there.

Thank God for waking me up. But the spirit of despondency is a relentless demon. Until you are completely aware of them as a demonic entity, there is no way you will be able to defend yourself from them completely. The spirit of despondency tried to get me again in 2011. I was so angry with my mother over something so trivial – trivial but when it involved my mother, it's enough to disturb my whole world. It was so bad that I got so mad at her that I took an entire bottle of Advil. As soon as I swallowed the entire bottle of pills, I suddenly felt total shame. I was already making the effort to get my faith back then but the awareness wasn't there yet. I felt absolute shame. I suddenly had a crystal-clear awareness that I had no right to kill myself. I realized I had no right to hurt my body. As my eyes were closing, I was begging the Lord's forgiveness. I was begging God to please wake me up in the morning. Fortunately, by God's mercy, I woke up the following morning energized. It was as if nothing happened the night before. I was in good spirits. Since that time, I never ever attempted to kill myself again although I was still suicidal – mentally, emotionally and psychologically but I just never attempted to hurt myself again. I could not forget the shame I felt and the realization that I had no right. I can only thank God for giving me that grace.

When I finally got my faith back in 2012, I was able to confess in Fatima, Portugal. It was my first time to confess face to face with a priest. He was an old man with blue eyes, and as soon as I confessed about my attempt to kill myself, I could see the sadness in his eyes – it's like seeing Jesus in person. He held my hand and gave me absolution for my sins. I remembered crying freely – released and free from the spirit of despondency. I didn't know about demons yet at that time, but after that confession, I had the firm commitment to never allow myself to be separated from God. Since that pilgrimage, I always find myself praying to God to never allow me to be separated from him.

When I confessed to an exorcist in Naga, Cebu after he processed me when I consulted him regarding my new helper that showed signs of being possessed during my father's birthday back in 2022, I was concerned if my fear to be separated from the Lord is a sin. He clarified with me why I was afraid. And I said, *"I don't know father – all I know is I cannot afford to ever be separated from God because without him, I know all will be lost."* I thought I was afraid because I lacked faith. Then father said, *"that is a grace April. Fear of losing the Lord – or fear of being separated from him because the alternative will be utter darkness is a grace. It's one of the gifts of the Holy Spirit."*

It is important to mention that the helper just arrived at my doorstep because another helper hired her without my permission. She was very young, pretty and looked so innocent. But shortly after our introduction, I learned that she was walking possessed. Earlier that day, I asked the Lord silently in my mind, when I will finally witness an actual physical possession. I am very familiar with mental, physical and psychological attacks but I have not quite witnessed an actual possession. Although I always suspected that I was possessed during the initial part of my Out of Body experience in Vietnam because I had four sets of huge claw marks on my back.

PORN NO MORE: Overcoming the Spirit of Lust

While I was able to overcome the spirit of despondency, the next demon God wanted me to overcome was the spirit of lust. Though I am not quite certain, which came first, my suicide attempt or my liberation from porn. It is important to note that getting liberated from certain spirits are never smooth because the enemy will never let go without a fight. Looking on hindsight, it was highly likely that my liberation from porn came before I overcame the spirit of despondency.

This is my story on pornography, or just porn for brevity. As a woman, especially at my stature, few would admit they watch porn. Mine started shortly after my best friend died. Grief is very dangerous. It took me over 20 years to finally accept the loss. But my grief was definitely what opened my door to the demonic. Back in the 90s, I was introduced to the World Wide Web (www). I had a cyber-best friend forever (bff) from New York City who introduced me to porn. He was an architect so he was teaching it to me graphically while we were long-distance. Since then, my porn collection had grown. More so while I was in New York City due to unlimited and super-fast internet. When I came home in the Philippines in 2008, I realized I was already an atheist. I can't recall exactly when I lost it but I know I was already losing my faith after Simone died.

Though I started faking having faith in 2009, I never really got my faith back until 2012.

But sometime in 2009 to 2011, where I was bombarded with severe depression and even made several suicidal attempts; one night, while I was watching porn, I suddenly felt sick – the porn I was watching was becoming so gross. I was totally so grossed out that I decided to delete my entire porn collection. As soon as I pressed DELETE, I literally felt a very huge weight or a weighted *presence* was lifted off of me. Do note, that at this time, I was still faithless – suicidal, in fact. I consulted an exorcist about this. I asked him, how did the Holy Spirit managed to reach me, at a moment where I still had no faith and I was in a very dark place? His answer was very simple but it was enough to make me cry.

> *"Simply, God's love does not and will not judge us. God moves in very mysterious ways, for us to be brought closer to Him."*

Resisting Heresy

After defeating the spirit of lust, God made me overcome the spirit of heresy. The person that got me to reading the bible was actually my friend Peachy. Peachy was a baptized Catholic who later turned protestant. But because of her, I decided to buy my first New International Version (NIV) Bible. I was so motivated that I committed the sin of spiritual gluttony – I was always overdoing my efforts and deluded myself that if I buy more bibles, it will add merit to my faith. But that's not correct. We cannot bribe our way to faith. It's never that simple.

It's also important to mention that back in 2007 or 2008, the reason why I had to come home was that my uncle (my father's brother), was suddenly dying of lung cancer. He was in charge of our manufacturing plant that I headed, and my father was also manifesting a bleeding colon. My uncle had very little time left. My aunt from Davao, out of desperation, contacted an exorcist. He wasn't an exorcist that cast out evil directly but what he does was pray – contemplative praying. He had a charism that can discern the source of the oppression in high definition. He said that while he was praying in Davao, it was so strong that the earth shook. True enough, there was a major earthquake that reached all the way to Cebu. Or maybe the earthquake happened in Cebu that reached Davao or something like that.

He was the very first exorcist I have ever met in my life. He asked my uncle a series of questions such as where was he over 20 years ago, when he was still single. My uncle said he was a treasure-hunt guide and there were a group of people who hired him to go treasure hunting in Samal Island, Davao. He said he never even got off the boat the entire time. But the exorcist explained that treasure hunting is a demonic activity and is extremely perilous because the spirits attached to the treasures are vehicles of the demonic. These are very angry and vengeful spirits because the reason why they are not liberated is because of their greed and fear that people will try to steal their treasures away. Since these are vengeful spirits, it will attack everyone. They are no longer living entities that has reason. These are unrested, angry souls with a bunch of demons attached to them.

The principle of contamination is quite simple, he explained. He made us imagine an invisible mud and imagine sitting on them but since we cannot see the mud as we move around, we transmit the mud everywhere. We even bring it at home. It is the very principle of disease contamination. Since it's been building up all those years, it crosses over the entire bloodline. He then asked my uncle if he knew what happened to the other passengers on the boat. My uncle said, they all died a violent death. And the exorcist said, "and you are the last one left". My uncle said, "that was a very long time ago." And the Exorcist said, "until it is cut, it will remain in the bloodline. You, your family, and relatives have to cut it." He gave us a series of very basic prayers that goes, *"Come Lord Jesus, Come into Our family, bless us, help us, Heal us"* and accompany it with the Holy Rosary as often as we can daily for as long as I can remember. We were all instructed to do it diligently.

Though I was still faithless, I was still afraid of demons so I was all too willing to pray what I have to pray in order to break the curse. I was much more driven by fear. I was already very fascinated with the topic even if I was afraid. I went to the bookstore and that was the first time I saw a book on Exorcism, written by Fr. Jocis Syquia. I scanned his book briefly and read on the part that when he gets very scared, he prays to the Blessed Virgin, and the enemy cannot simply stand it. Let's hold this part for now and will get back to this on a nightmare I had in 2011.

Since my friend, Peachy, is a protestant, it was but natural for her to discourage me from praying to Mama Mary – but somehow, I really didn't feel comfortable abandoning Mama Mary. I was already actively praying mechanically, like how I used to before. I also resumed to talking to God directly like how I used to before. I asked the Lord, "Lord, I know

I have offended you so much already for allowing myself to lose faith in you, an atheist no less, and now that I am making this effort to come back, I don't want to offend you by committing a mistake. I don't trust the honesty of my thoughts. Kindly speak to me, before I go any deeper on this if it is okay for me to pray to Mama Mary? Lord, please speak to me in a language I can understand." Surely, God did.

Sometime in 2011, I decided to take a nap at noon time just an hour before we will launch an International Film Festival I founded with Peachy along with my former professor and another Rotarian. I remember waking up with a demon on my bed. The experience was very similar to when I had a sleep paralysis back in college. This time, it was not dark. It was very bright. It was still in the afternoon. It wasn't a dream. The problem was, I couldn't move. I tried to pray the "Lord's Prayer" but I couldn't – I tried several times to utter the words but I just couldn't move my mouth. I remember really trying very hard in my dream.

The demon in front of me had this deformed evil face – it's almost like what we see in horror movies. He was initially smiling playfully but the moment he realized I couldn't pray, his smile turned sinister. Suddenly, that one demon became two. They were at the edge of the bed and we're about to come to me. Do note that I thought I was dreaming but suddenly, I *remembered* while I was dreaming the book by Fr. Syquia. I remembered that when he got very scared, he prayed to Mama Mary. Imagine, my eyes were closed when I prayed "*Hail Mary, Full of Grace the Lord is with you....*" And didn't stop praying when I opened my eyes. There was no interruption. I was fully aware of my prayer from sleep state to wake state.

When I stood up, I looked at the mirror and I saw that one of my eyes was red. I realized that when I was trying very hard to pray the Lord's Prayer, I was truly physically making the effort to do so that the blood vessels in one of my eyes exploded. That explained my red eye. It was really red that when I went to the launching, everybody was asking what happened to my eyes.

I was initially disturbed why I couldn't pray the Lord's Prayer. Then I remembered asking the Lord about Mama Mary. That was my confirmation. God didn't allow me to pray the Lord's Prayer so I will be forced to remember Mama Mary. That was surely an emphatic yes. I knew that was from God because I never told anyone about my prayer. There was no way the demons had access to my thoughts unless I told someone about it. Demons are also afraid of the Blessed Virgin and it's very well documented among all exorcists' notes, especially by the late Fr. Gabriel Amorth, the former chief exorcist in the Vatican. At this time, I didn't know about Fr. Amorth and the principle behind spiritual warfare yet. At this time, it would seem I already got my faith back but the awareness, wasn't there yet.

That day was my initial confirmation that the *Catholicism* was the direction I had to take because there is no other religion back then that acknowledge the Blessed Virgin Mary. It was enough to make me confident at that time that I was heading on the right direction.

Allow me to describe how tumultuous it was as I was trying to get my faith back – the feelings of emptiness became even more pronounced. Instead of getting better, things were getting absolutely worse. It is very hard to think clearly at that time. The feeling was akin to being poured freezing water that simply doesn't stop pouring. You feel so alone. The loneliness was deafening. My daily routine of coming home to an empty house – just living on my own, repeating the same routine day in and day out, without any particular direction or purpose in mind, and not being able to see any possible change in sight, I asked the Lord, *"Lord, is this how it's going to be for me forever? Will things ever change for me?"*

Shortly after that earnest conversation I had with God, I was in my office one time– talking to a graphic designer because I was planning to start a "signature gifting business," which later turned into a travel business, one of my dad's engineers bought a puppy. She was embarrassed that a puppy was running into me and apologized. I told her how cute her puppy was and she explained that she is choosing a puppy for her daughter. And I just pleasantly asked her if I could see them as well. When they brought up one of the puppies, I made contact with one of them.

That was my first experience of *love at first sight*. I named her Arkigirl. She was a mixed-breed of Shih Tzu and whatever. I just suddenly stood up, forgot about everybody else, took the puppy and left. My dad ended up paying for my puppy because I just left without looking back. Why am I mentioning my dog here? Because this dog has managed to transform me in ways no human being ever could. I made a lot of mistakes bringing her up. Her personality now is exactly the reflection of me when she met me. She bites when she is touched. She doesn't like to be made fun of. She is grumpy but she is quite endearing for as long as you don't touch her. That was so me when I met her. I have significantly changed since then but Arkigirl is evidence of what I used to be. Because it hurt me so much that I cannot help her when she is sick, that I cannot make her feel better – I made certain that I will not make the same mistakes I made with her to my other dogs. I made certain that none of my other dogs will bite. I literally had to change myself. When I used to yell, and scream when I get mad, Arkigirl would growl at me, while New York and all my other dogs will hide from me. They didn't need words for me to realize how awful I was. They helped me become aware of myself. They helped me become aware of my temper. Since then, I watched myself by the way they responded to me. I learned to love because there is nothing, I can do to them but love them. Even though, they cannot talk, but I felt their affection. I felt their love and loyalty. It was probably all I really needed during that time. A companion.

Going back to my non-profit, I decided to expand our program. There was an Australian documentary filmmaker who volunteered to document our programs ever since, and it was very well edited. I thought, it would be great if we can showcase them in a film festival. Unfortunately, there wasn't any local film festivals that we know of yet at that time. So, I consulted my classmate in Stanford, Aarti, who was an award-winning documentary filmmaker from India to help me. She suggested that I should start an International "documentary" film festival in Cebu. And this was how the idea of founding *Cebu International Documentary Film Festival (CIDFF)* came to be. She suggested the profile of the board of directors that I needed to gather, in order for the festival to work. I followed her suggestion to a tee. Since I didn't know of any filmmakers yet at that time, except for one documentary filmmaker from Manila, but when I reached out to her, she dismissed my idea as she described the very delicate structure of the film industry in the Philippines. As usual, I never take no for an answer. We needed a platform for our programs to be showcased. I got all of my board members from my fellow Rotarians. We successfully launched our first edition in 2012 with over 30 film submissions from across the world. I engaged my old I-House friend from South Africa, and hired a film consultant from India, whose involvement in CIDFF got her an important position in her country that will allow her to represent her country in Cannes. Of which I also went the following year. I would represent CIDFF in various Film Festivals and Film Markets such as Hong Kong, Dubai, Hawaii, Kathmandu, Holland, and in Barcelona too.

Because I simply cannot serve two masters, Omnilogy just died a natural death. I had to focus on the festival that I worked with full-time, with zero salary, and which my family had significantly helped financed for six straight years, with zero ROI and it wasn't tax-deductible either. I eventually took an indefinite leave of absence from the board leadership in 2016 so I can focus on myself. I was so burnt out and was extremely broke. Extremely. I didn't know what I was going to do since I have been in the non-profit industry for about 10 years.

Despite my super broke status, I still spent the next three years focusing on my triathlon training – the years where I started with my reparation, purely thru the guidance of the Holy Spirit. I didn't have full awareness of what I was doing but I was significantly offering reparations during my physical training. I spent these entire years getting to know my capacity to feel pain, and learning about endurance. These were the years where I felt, I was getting to know

"Mama Mary" more intimately through this painful sport. Somewhere along the way, I just figured out that if I pray the Rosary while I am training, I could endure my training. I also figured out that I could concentrate on praying if I am training. I didn't like training in groups – I always preferred training alone because it made me feel closer to God. I got to speak to God in the silence of my thoughts while my body is suffering a beating. Knowledge-wise, I was still far from knowing the faith but intimacy-wise, I was already building my spiritual muscles during this time. I was learning a lot about myself and the amount of physical pain I was capable of enduring for as long as I am offering it to God.

TRIATHLON FINISH
IN PURGATORY

Tick Tock

Tick tock tick tock
Time ticking tick tock
Hearts beating, dum dum dum
Slow slow slow sound
Fade fade fade away

Can I see a smile?
From a silhouette hind?
Like a rollercoaster ride
 in the cloudless sky?
The moon peeps in,
Like a colorless gin
What's there to gaze?
In a shadowy blaze?

Hush hush hush
be still little heart

There's always a tough shot,
Tomorrow's another light,

Goodnight little darling
There's gold in the morning
The sun will rise high
Like a featherless flight

Life's like that
Like a kick in the shin
Laugh like a bat
That kicks like a fin

Rise rise high
Will always make sense
Sleep sleep tight
The dark won't stay tense

Tock tick tock
Time will get past
This strange little hump
Will go without thump

Good night dim sky!
Ride the night by
Dream dream away
The sadness good bye

I wrote below shortly after my out of body experience while attempting to complete a 70.3 mile Ironman race in Vietnam. I thought the experience was pretty bizarre and tried to document everything I could process while

Out of Body. It was a scary experience but I felt a divine purpose for it.

"During IM 70.3 Vietnam Race in March 2017, I collapsed. I can't remember when, how and where. To this day, I have no recollection of what happened to me...except my dreams. Dreams that seemed too real to be just a dream. It was a nightmare.

I was just running, approximately 500 meters to the finish line; I could see the flags from a distance. I was so near then suddenly; I woke up in darkness. The first thing I noticed was I was floating and not attached to my body. I recall saying, "I do not exist!"

I recall vomiting endlessly behind a vehicle then I was inside the ambulance. I couldn't stop vomiting. I remember feeling dirty from my vomit. I remember feeling excruciating pain all throughout my body. I remember screaming in pain on the top of my lungs and losing complete control of myself. I remember a man looking down at me kindly but extremely worried. I could only look at him. I couldn't say anything because the pain in my body was paralyzing. Suddenly, I was in the dark. I remember my last arguments with people. Certain people. I remember feelings of resentments. Then I felt each of my bones breaking. For real. From the edge of my fingers to my toenails. I felt my thighs being spread apart, almost being torn but there was nobody there. It was just me. I felt exposed and dirty. Then I could recall the words of people who said, there is no God. See April? If there is a God, why does he let you feel this much pain? Then I recall believing. I recall asking, maybe God is an imperfect God. Maybe he did not intend to trust a human any responsibility because each time he does, they fail him constantly. Maybe he doesn't have control. I remember again the persistent, never-ending pain. I remembered people saying why, if there is a God, is there life? Does life really exist? What for??? I remember agreeing that maybe life is just a consciousness and that there is really no God. I remember understanding people who are possessed and people who fought evil. I remember looking at those people who looked at me with pity and say, you don't know what's in here. You can say that because you don't know what's in here. You don't know pain that has no end. You don't know pain that doesn't calm down. In that moment, I said to myself, I can understand why there are those who do not believe. They have reached a level of consciousness.... this consciousness where the God that we believed in, seems cruel. I remember pride. Even to demand to be good is still pride. I remembered being trapped. No matter what argument, I am doomed to fail. I remembered feeling trapped. I remembered feeling so helpless. I couldn't feel my existence. I couldn't feel myself. In that moment I believed that maybe life exist simply because it just does. I remembered just simply accepting it as it is but I was in so much pain. Then a part of me continued to ask, why am I still feeling this much pain? Why are people who's looking at me not feeling what I'm feeling? Am I the only one? And then a voice would say, they will get there, to where you are and it circles back again to the vast universe of God. I asked again, why does life exist if there is no God? What for? The repeated answer was, "consciousness". But then I asked, why do we have "consciousness"? Just so we can experience love, joy, and this ultimate pain? The voice said, so he can hurt you because he is a cruel God. He isn't really a God. He is just lonely that's why he created you. I suddenly remembered memories of falling in love, memories of feelings of kindness, gratitude, memories of feelings of compassion. Then I asked, if it is just consciousness, why do we need to be born? Why is it that when I was alive, the God that I know demanded for me to do good? If he is a cruel God, why do I remember the demand to forgive and show mercy? What does he have to gain by me forgiving and giving mercy? Then everything I learned about God and the bible started to make sense. At that moment, I felt a sudden compassion for humanity that I even felt mercy to the Evil one whom I was arguing to. I realized how it is incapable to feel compassion, understanding, love and mercy. I realized then how powerful those words actually are. It was the moment I started to realize I am coming back to life.

The Bible, indeed, is the blue print to a life of consciousness – the consciousness that I'm talking about is the consciousness that God wants to share with us. "We were created in his image and likeness". Heaven and eternal life are not a place but a consciousness...a consciousness of compassion, of understanding, of transcending our bodily wants and needs.

I realized why people closest to God are attacked. Because WE RESIST! We are broken down inside, tortured inside, because we put up a fight. I recall why people who has gone thru what I've gone thru now will choose not to believe because to continue to believe would mean to continue feeling this pain. I also realized and finally understood why there are Saints and how they are indeed God's jewels in his crown because they share God's unconditional love for humanity and their willingness to share the pain of Jesus Christ. It is there that I fully understood why Jesus Christ had to die for mankind - to demonstrate the ultimate purpose of man being incarnate. To demonstrate that physical pain and all kinds of pain is not to be feared but embraced in order to realize the hugeness of the values of love, compassion, mercy, understanding and patience. There is eternal life with God but we have to earn our place there ONLY if we can love each other as how God does, as how Jesus Christ demonstrated it to us. This is the purpose of the bible - to spell everything we need to know to enter God's kingdom. I also saw glimpses of what separates people from God. I saw graphic images that demonstrates the obstruction. It was so strange. The language, the communication was not verbal yet I get the message so clearly in the absence of words. I saw a smokescreen, like fingers interlocking preventing human beings from seeing God and all his goodness. But God was always there. He never left. He was always there. It was just us who couldn't see them and I understood about generational open doors that created those smokescreens. How did I reckon all of this? It was like seeing or watching a silent film...no words, just pictures, vintages, not the whole scene.

It is then I realized the meaning of death. At this point, I thought I died. I realized acceptance. I thought, when we cry when people we love dies, we can't accept the concept of death. We have fear when death isn't to be feared. Death is a transition of consciousness. Death is indeed just a metamorphosis. We transcend into a consciousness with God. That is if we are certain that the consciousness is about absolute humility, understanding, compassion, generosity, kindness, and purity. When we realize the essence of God's design of life, the perfection of his consciousness, we die. But yet I am alive, why? Perhaps my consciousness of God's wisdom is not stable enough. I did recall asking for a second chance. Thank you, God, for this second chance.

When I opened my eyes, I still couldn't feel my existence. I felt invisible. I felt like I have no body, no name. Then a doctor was asking for my name. She seemed angry. Then suddenly, a kind person came. A girl who kept on smiling at me, asking for my name. She was comforting me. She said, you are okay. Don't worry, you are okay. They asked again, what's your name?"

"I can do all things through Christ
who gives me strength."
(Philippians 4:13)

In all my life growing up as Catholic since kindergarten, this thought process of "...whatever you receive means nothing after death. It's what you have given that matters," never registered to me until I died in Vietnam back in 2017. While I always learned since kindergarten that Christ is our Lord and Savior, it was only when I went under and out there, in space, without my incarnate human flesh, that I truly understood the significance of the incarnate body of Christ, and inadvertently, my own. Thank you, God, for my life.

When I woke up in darkness, and in terrible absolute unceasing pain (the memory of which still traumatizes me and made me cringe), what made the pain irrelevant was memories of good deeds that I have done. Memories of virtues i.e. me giving mercy, me giving compassion, me giving kindness are like real life companions that made all the pain irrelevant.

I understood, without equivocation, that it is only through our incarnate human flesh can man achieve purification – a privilege only afforded to man. A gift, only given to man alone. It is only thru this lifetime can one achieve salvation and nothing else. I recall that in all my life where I felt insecure because of my birthmark, waking up and getting back to life where I thought I had already died made me see myself in a whole new light. I remember looking at myself in the mirror, touching my face and telling myself, *"I love you. Forgive me for all the years I tried to disown you, rejected you and even killed you. You are the only one who can give me a chance to get me a spot in heaven. Thank you, Lord for giving me this body."* I have never been more grateful of my life because of what happened to me in Vietnam.

I understood, without any doubt that Jesus Christ is life. Jesus Christ personified the essence of our lives. Jesus Christ demonstrated in the most literal way how we can achieve salvation and it is to live exactly like him. I finally understood why we pray to saints and it's not to worship them like gods but to honor them because they allowed themselves to suffer like Christ for love of God, which also equates to our love of humanity – and they are not reversible nor interchangeable; we are only truly able to love humanity when we love God. It is extremely difficult to love humanity with all our flaws, betrayal, dishonesty, and weaknesses to resist evil. This is why we need to *love God* first and foremost – the total surrender borne from love, mercy and compassion for God's greater glory. They are jewels in God's crown. We were created in God's image and likeness and it's the saints that truly lived up to it. Heaven, is to achieve that sense of unconditional love, mercy and compassion for all souls including those that hurt us. Yes, many are called but few are chosen.

I still have so many questions that sometimes, I'm afraid to ask since God always answer me so accurately, especially when I asked him to speak to me in a language I can understand. He surely does answer. If you are uncertain of so many things and are conflicted spiritually, ask God directly and ask that he speaks to you "*in a language you can understand*" but remember to be strong – all the time because his answers will not be a walk in the park. Be prepared to be shaken. I am always shaken to the core each time he answers. But I asked for it.

FINDING MY RELIGION

A few years ago, I always thought the whole world was Catholic. Even when I used to travel then, I never really noticed the large reality that being Catholic is NOT an option readily available to anyone. I always thought that those who are Protestants or atheists etc. were Catholic at some point. But no. There are many who were born without any faith. Though I grew up in a Catholic environment, for a long time, I didn't seem to realize how valuable it was until I lost it when I moved to New York City. It was there where I met people totally absent of faith but mind yeah, I was very good friends with them. One of them even have family who were atheists up to the 3rd generation. If any, it was something that I found spiritually disturbing. I have made friends with people who told me, "There is no God April. The concept of God is only for crazy people". One of them spoke of it with absolute confidence and certainty. I was speechless. I felt stupid.

Along the way, God sent me angels who invited me out for bible study yet I would find myself feeling "weirded" out by it. There were many beautiful souls who would have made great life partners but I chose to look at the unattainable. I was attracted to the unattainable. I seem to have an attraction towards the unattainable. For a while, I was totally, absolutely happy. Like I said, I never ever thought of myself as an attractive or beautiful woman but when I moved to International House, I started wondering if I am. I remember being in an elevator with a good-looking French man with a very kind face. I just smiled at him before I got off and told him "Have a great evening!" The following night, while I was at the fourth floor lounge reading, he suddenly came in and said, "Hi, my name is Nicholas. I am sorry if this will sound strange but since I saw you yesterday, I couldn't seem to get you out of my mind and this has never happened to me before." I was absolutely shocked. It was so romantic and if it was written in romantic books or screenplay, it would certainly be a fantastic scene. I didn't know what to say. And his reply was even so much better, he said, "I know this sound strange to you and I don't expect you to respond but I am wondering if we can go out sometime. I mean, not tonight but maybe we can talk about when later." I was really speechless and I remember nodding.

He wasn't irritating or "kulit" a Filipino term for people who are too persistent. He was quite patient and polite. He was actually a lawyer and was very refined. But at that time, I wouldn't recognize a diamond even if I was staring in one. I took him for granted.

Before him, I was actually asked out by a German saxophonist and composer to watch an orchestra at the Carnegie Hall. I have never been to an orchestra, and let alone, Carnegie Hall, which I knew at that time to be the Mecca concert hall of classical musicians in New York City, if not the world. That was New York, after all. So, I went with him. He wasn't my type so over dinner, to avoid encouraging him further, I decided to eat in a Chinese restaurant and ordered all my favorite dishes. I was hoping he would get turned off by my huge appetite. I was also very casual with the way I ate. I was neither prim nor proper. I was just behaving like "one of the guys" like I always do with my high school swim buddies or college classmates, who were mostly male. He laughed and told me, "I love a woman with a good appetite." That disturbed me more than I felt complimented. I avoided him since.

During my birthday, which I celebrated at the pub with my floor mates who were so sweet enough to surprise me with a party, cakes and all, Nicholas – the French lawyer came. We talked and it was so timely that when he asked me when I would be free to go out on a date with him, the Danish guy was suddenly seated next to me. Perhaps I liked the feeling of being asked out in front of him, I decided to say yes to the French lawyer, which the Danish guy also heard. Nicholas was also very sweet in asking me for my favorite food – and at that time, I was crazy for sushi – all kinds of sushi. The following day, he took me to Mikado with a full array of sushi. He was really the best date anyone can ever ask for. He was intelligent, entertaining, articulate, kind and so many more. As we asked for the check, I knew how expensive the place was so I was about to pay half even if it was him who asked me out, but then, he gently put his hand over mine and said, "If you don't mind April, can I take this?"

I was really impressed at how gentle he was. We strolled along the city and he had his hand on my hips. It was a sweet gesture but that scared me. I got those familiar cold feet again. I couldn't wait to be separated from him and went home. He thought it was a very good date and asked me when our next would be. I told him I will give him a call, and I never did. That was the one and only time that we ever went out on a date. We would say hi to each other when we cross path. He would ask again, but I would always refuse or come up with an excuse not to. I thought he got over it already. He was never ever unkind to me. Never. Ever. In fact, even when the Danish guy has left, and I would get so wild in the pub, talking or chatting to a lot of guys. I would often get loud. People would talk negatively against me, especially women. Nicholas, would hear them talk bad about me, and he would always come to my defense. He would tell them, "April is a great person. We used to go out together and she is very nice". He told one of my female friends that, that was also heard by those people who talked bad about me. When my friend told me about it, I was so confused. I was confused because I didn't really value him. He remained nice to me for as long as I can remember and all I could feel was frustration why I cannot seem to reciprocate, when he totally deserved all the love and care from any woman – of which, I don't ever recall him approaching or dating for the entire duration that he was in I-House. Up until I was expelled from my university, it was only during that time that I regretted not being with him. It was also the time that he grew distant with me. It's like he has gotten over me, finally.

When I don't care about being with any guy, its usually the time that I keep attracting them. There was this I-House trustee event, where I often get so nervous and conscious. I read a book by Dale Carnegie, that was given to me by my ex-boyfriend, *"How to Win Friends and Influence People."* That night, I thought I would give it a try. I was with this couple, who were also trustees of the house, and the husband was a former ambassador, so I decided to speak with his wife by simply asking her questions about herself. I was just listening and kept the questions coming based on her stories. The next thing I knew, she called her husband and his son, who was with her and told them how fascinating I am. I was confused because all I actually did was asked her questions. I don't recall sharing anything about myself – I just kept asking her questions about herself. The next thing I knew, his son asked me out on a date, in the W, a very high-end and posh hotel in Manhattan. As usual, I always get cold feet. Always. I went out with him but I don't recall communicating with him after that date. Same with what I did with the German guy, with Nicholas, and same with all other guys that I went out with in NYC, other than Danish guy and John.

I recall a conversation with my aunt in the Philippines when she asked me what is it that I loved about New York City. I told her, "I loved it here because NOBODY CARES Tita!". She suddenly became silent on the other line and told me, well – "if being with people who doesn't care makes you happy then...what can I say?"

At the peak of that happiness, before the Danish guy left, I remembered God. I remember asking God, "is this for real my Lord? Is it possible to feel and experience this exquisite joy? I am only 26. I was friends with everyone. I was in love. I felt on top of the world. Is it possible to be already at a point where I can't ask for anything more?"

Suddenly, one by one, the curtains fell.

Looking back, I knew now, that being happy is not always the end all of everything. I asked the question because though I was happy – I was alone in that happiness. I didn't share it with anyone. Though they were my friends and perhaps I made them happy too with my presence, but I didn't exactly share a life with them to include their sorrows. To be in a relationship with people – we need to be able to live and experience joy even in their state of sorrow.

Then a few years after, I found out that an atheist friend of mine just converted to become a Baptist, another embraced her being Catholic though she was baptized, she never really practiced. The entire time I thought I was absent of faith; people were seeing faith in me. I used to wear a rosary bracelet that my mom gave me before I left for NYC and it was just a force of habit that compelled me to wear them. My friend, who went back to Catholicism, asked for it and I was surprised that she even noticed them. Months after, she told me she could already recite the Holy Rosary. Hearing this, it was like something in me was being re-awakened. Though I didn't fully realize it then but now I knew, I was being called back. Though the awareness that I already lost my faith, wasn't there yet let alone realizing that I needed to go back. I seem to get a constant reminder of that time. That time that I took my faith for granted while many so labored to seek it and find it. And when they finally did, they embraced it with all their might and heart.

There are times where one has to learn to surrender to a higher being. I agree that it isn't something that can be forced on to anyone. It comes, when it comes. I am brought up a Catholic but I never really appreciated it until I tried the *"I can do-and solve everything on my own--relying on no one -but my own self and mind thing"* and it wasn't that much fun. I've taken the cynical route while deluding myself into believing it was cool. I gained nothing but lost plenty. There's only darkness there. Believing doesn't mean there's no pain nor heartache or no doubts. Believing helps one accept reality, and embrace the pain instead of getting overwhelmed by fear. It's like a muscle. We just have to keep on working at it. It doesn't hold by just waiting for the guava (or apple) to fall on our mouth. It's a struggle to believe simply because we are human. It's not a walk in the park to keep one's faith contrary to the popular belief that believing is a coward's way out. It never is. This is why former atheists like myself, who have tried what total darkness is (when we are absent of faith), get sensitive when criticized about our faith in God, because we know how it felt to be without him.

It's not easy to be a believer, especially for those who have tried letting go of one's faith. It gets harder and I guess that's the price of free will rather than completely surrendering. The more we struggle, the easier it gets to believe and when you're in the zone - there's a sense of clarity that is just beyond words. And I want to protect that clarity as others who have it wants to protect it too. I yearn for that sense of clarity as others yearn for it too.

And so, we pray and inspire our hearts to keep watch for any miracle that may happen. Very often, we see it and it strengthens that sense of clarity. It is very hard to acquire but very well worth it once you have it. It is also very difficult to be a believer since being close to God would also make me visible to something very evil. Since evil, were once angels in their nature; they always find a way to find an open door in my life. Often times, they open the doors closest to us - our family.

My family has always been my biggest challenge. My source of insecurity. In my previous chapters, I talked about a very lonely childhood within my family since I've always been on the receiving end of my siblings' jealousy, and my mother's most "favorite" child (pun intended). Although, I have learned to forgive the past but it gets difficult when the very family that deprived me of such emotional security keep their doors open to evil. This has been my most difficult challenge of all - a challenge that surpasses all other challenges I've overcome in my life. I have overcome my desire to love and be loved by the man I loved. I have overcome the feeling of loneliness and embraced my aloneness. I have overcome my feelings of frustrations, regrets and disappointments and embraced my higher purposes instead.

I used to blame God for every little problem I feel towards my life but since I got my faith back, I am struggling to keep my dignity for God. Although I know what I must do to overcome this most difficult source of insecurity, I remain vulnerable. Having said that, I can't emphasize enough that to keep our faith intact and authentic is the most difficult challenge of all.

God doesn't spoon feed. When I ask for strength, he shows me immediately what it takes to be strong. When I ask for the grace of patience and humility, he shows me what it takes to be patient and to be humble. I find myself failing him all the time. The challenge of being a Christian is to have the humility and patience to be like Christ - to be willing to feel pain and offer it to him - to be willing to forgive those who hurt us to our core and demonstrate how we love God more than we love our human family. Yes, hating our loved ones and refusing to forgive them is an act that shows we don't love God enough. I understand this being a Christian and admittedly, the struggle is real and it will remain a struggle until the end of our lives.

Pride is my open door. Pride is a powerful demon. Pride is Lucifer. Why does God allow these demons to test me? Why does he let me experience so much pain? Each time I ask, I am reminded that I wanted to make myself worthy of him. Again, is this what it means to believe? To suffer? And the answer is -yes. God showed it by allowing his only begotten son to die on the cross.

And when I find myself crying in anger each time I entertain the story that my own mother was rejecting me while always choosing to favor all my other siblings, I then remember, how many times have I rejected God by refusing to forgive?

Finding one's religion isn't something that one is supposed to escape to but it's a place where one is compelled to face one's reality and accept it. Then one might wonder, is there ever happiness when one believes or is it all just suffering? And my answer is, for as long as I am unable to firmly close my open doors, there will always be suffering. For as long as the entire world keep their doors open to evil, we can never guarantee a life without suffering. This is what it feels like to be in hell - a life filled with so many open doors to evil.

Then one might say, if that's the case, I'd rather choose not to believe. If I'm just going to hell because I don't have the strength to close my open doors, I might as well not believe and enjoy whatever time left, I have in this world. I'd say that's a fair choice if one is unable to realize the true pain of hell. God's gift to me is discernment. I am much too aware of my pain. I have no strength to lie or pretend that I can choose to not feel pain. Because of this, I know I don't want to be in hell and if there's a slight chance or opportunity for me to be saved, I'll take it even if all I have is hope.

I don't believe that psychologists or psychiatrists know the way to happiness for with their jobs, it is simply dishonest of them to claim that they are happy. As a human being, it is simply impossible for one to not be affected by the pain of another no matter how well one rationalizes it. It's simply impossible. What they did develop is the ability to justify and reinterpret their emotions in countless probabilities such as to have the ability to be indifferent. Then, they are able to draw a story of happiness in their minds to prevent themselves from feeling anything remotely close to any form of pain.

Without faith in a higher being to offer all these sufferings to, that suffering will circulate. By offering, it isn't simply done by saying it, but by actually doing something such as making the conscious effort of transforming ourselves and overcoming our self-defeating behaviors that causes us to offend God. The act of offering one's suffering comes with the fact that one has embraced those pains, sharing it with Jesus Christ.

God's presence is so pronounced in that moment of offering. You will feel his love. The love that you realize at that moment is so certain, absolute and precise. That love is joy, which is so much deeper than happiness. People who truly have faith that is firm and true, knows exactly what I am talking about. The pain and suffering transform into a love that is so beautiful. The pain will actually cease to be so. The relationship between love and suffering is so thin. They are somewhat intertwined. Each time I truly embrace it, offer it, it's like something in me grows stronger and that something is faith. Faith is the most priceless gift God has given mankind as well as our propensity to make mistakes and capacity to transform. As they say, "to err is human, to forgive is divine".

I observed that all people starting and belonging in religions away from Christianity brings people closer to God in his time, one step at a time-- especially those furthest away from him. Religions of the world are not in competition of each other. It is our pride that make it seem it is. It is the game the demons are making us play to keep us divided from each other.

One thing I realized that I observed to be consistently true is that all religions if originally starting from outside the Catholic faith, is a stepping stone towards God. All religions. It means, God is calling you home. If you are an atheist and you become Islam, Protestant, Born Again, etc. - you are being called closer to God. Eventually, in God's time, God will bring you home. You can trust that. This is covered in the **CCC: Part One: 28,** "*In many ways, throughout history down to the present day, men have given expression to their quest for God in their religious beliefs and behaviors: in their prayers, sacrifices, rituals, meditations, and so forth. These forms of religious expression, despite the ambiguities they often bring with them, are so universal that one might call man a religious being.*" But in **CCC:**

Part One: 35, *"…. Man's faculties make him capable of coming to a knowledge of the existence of a personal God. But for man to be able to enter into real intimacy with him, God willed both to reveal himself to man and to give him the grace of being able to welcome this revelation in faith."*

Similarly, it's also further validated in the Second Vatican Council that, *"…the Church considers all goodness and truth found in these religions as a preparation for the Gospel"* (**Lumen Gentium 16**). It is therefore, important to note, that while we acknowledge that each religion is "not" in competition of each other as long as you believe in God, Catholics must never compromise our faith.

Being a Christian is already a manifestation of knowledge of the truth. Being a Christian in accordance to the Catholic faith is humanity's ultimate destination of faith in order for us to be saved. The principle of secularism as stated in the Vatican II does not mean we <u>compromise</u> our faith at all, but we open our doors, as an extension of God's mercy.

If one recalls in the Old Testament, God's firm command to Abraham, down to Isaac and so forth to not marry a Canaanite. It took me a while to understand why God was very firm on that – it's because God wanted to protect his chosen line from spiritual contamination, of which King Solomon has significantly failed to protect. But because of God's absolute mercy, God changed all of that when he entered humanity thru his only son, Jesus Christ. He wiped the slate clean wherein he established that we *"Love our Enemies."*

On the reversal, if you are coming from the Catholic faith and you are called to become protestants, born again

Christians, Islam, Torah, etc. – I am sorry to say but it's the devil calling you away from God because that is a mortal sin called, *Incredulity*. See *CCC: Part Three: 2089*,

> "*Incredulity* is the neglect of revealed truth or the willful refusal to assent to it. "*Heresy* is the obstinate post-baptismal denial of some truth which must be believed with divine and catholic faith, or it is likewise an obstinate doubt concerning the same; *apostasy* is the total repudiation of the Christian faith; *schism* is the refusal of submission to the Roman Pontiff or of communion with the members of the Church subject to him."

It will be way harder to return to God than those who never knew God as a Catholic to begin with. So be very careful before you dabble on leaving Catholicism. The truth is self-evident. Christianity is not political, nor a question of superiority. Each religion serves a purpose and why they are allowed to vary, is still part of God's design. Having said that, people who grew up in a Christian environment bears more responsibility than those who didn't because a Christian is supposed to know the truth. When a Christian moves away from God, it is harder for them to return – since disobedience driven by pride or unforgiveness is the reason why they moved away to begin with. This is actually the sin of heresy and apostasy, as described above in *CCC*. They know the truth and yet still chose to turn away. It will be harder to return but it doesn't mean it is hard because God doesn't want us back, but because pride will not let go so easily. Don't underestimate pride– it will deceive you for as long as you let it. Pride will constantly make you feel ashamed. Pride will constantly make you feel guilty. Pride will not let you see that God's hand was always there for you to hold on to. A Christian knows the truth and only needs true humility to remember. It takes courage to be humble enough to forgive yourself for letting go. You'll know when you have forgiven yourself. You'll wake up one day and you just remember the love you always had. Like the parable of the prodigal son – we will all return to him, in God's time.

Being Catholic is not a mere religion. Other religions (in political terms) were created to divide humanity. Catholicism is the opposite. It's called Catholic, from the Greek word, "*Katholikos*" which means "universal" because it unites all of humanity in one faith. As Christians, it is our job to stay strong in our faith so we can help save the whole of humanity from eternal demise. There is a reason why we are Catholics. It is never by accident. We carry the responsibility to help bring the whole world who are far away back to God thru prayers and imitation of Jesus Christ – literally, from birth to death in the best way possible as willed by no less than God, himself.

To be Catholics mean we believe in "Jesus Christ". There is no other meaning to being Catholic but a Christian. But why we are called Catholic is to emphasize that Christianity is for everyone. It's not an exclusive religion. It was never designed to be exclusive. What makes it seem exclusive is the fact that when one is Catholic, one has to submit to the *Authority of the Roman Catholic Church*. Obedience is very critical. Disobedience is the greatest sin committed by Adam & Eve and over the course of the Old Testament, people kept on failing. Before Aaron and his sons were instituted by God as priests, people even their enemies could still hear the voice of God. But because of the sinfulness of man, we were no longer worthy to speak to him directly. Our sinfulness has totally separated us from God. But since God's mercy is so infinite, he gave us opportunities to repair the wounds we created that offended God by offering sacrifices thru the priests he instituted. But, instead of getting better, we grew more sinful that no amount of animal sacrifices would suffice. Yet again, God's mercy is infinite for he himself, became human. This is why God gave us Jesus Christ, God in his human form, to which he demonstrated that while his human form died, his divine nature lived forever, of which, we have to remember that we were all created in God's image and likeness. Jesus Christ commanded Peter to build his church, which is the Roman Catholic Church. Why? Because the **Authority of the Roman Catholic Church** is the **Authority of God**. God designed this to be so. In **CCC: Part Three: 1918**: *"There is no authority except from God, and those authorities that exist have been instituted by God"* (Rom 13:1)

And if Jesus Christ represents the Authority of God, as he is God made man, and he gave authority to his apostles to build his church, doesn't it follow that the Authority of the Roman Catholic Church, is the Authority of God? This world is just a staging venue. This is not the destination. The destination follows after death, as Jesus emphasized in the book of **John 18:36**, *".... My kingdom does not belong to this world"* This life - prepares us for that destination - that life that has no death.

Why do I emphasize "Roman" in the Catholic Church? Read the Book of **Matthew 16: 18-19**, when Jesus commanded Peter, *"And I also say to you that you are Peter, and upon this rock, I will build my church; and the gates of Hades will not overpower it."* Who is Peter now? Where can we find Peter? There is only one answer. In the Vatican, which used to be one and the same with Rome. While many Protestants (formerly Catholics) would love to cite many bible verses, but the mere fact that they are separated from the only church founded by Jesus, make them susceptible to the influence of the evil one. Why? Because of disobedience. It is important to emphasize that without the Roman Catholic Church, there wouldn't be any Holy Bible. That is actually an indisputable historical fact. Jesus left us a church and the seven (7) sacraments that can only be performed by the apostles, not just the bible – see *Matthew 28:18-19*, *"All authority in heaven and on earth has been given to me. Go, therefore, make disciples of all nations; baptize them in the name of the Father, the Son and the Holy Spirit,"* …. So, what does it mean if God left us a Church, not just the bible? It means the church is the only authority that can interpret the bible and that interpretation is stipulated in the doctrine. Only the Catholic Church has apostolic succession. When we say doctrine, we are referring to what is written in the *Catechism of the Roman Catholic Church*. It is very easy to copy and paste the references and just search for this online. They go together with the Holy Bible. It cannot just be one or the other, it has to be both. And we have to remember always that these laws will never change. It is the exact same law yesterday, today, and tomorrow until forever. It will never change. But because God is merciful, there are pastoral considerations that the church will consider provided that they don't violate both "scripture and doctrine". This is critical that we must know both. It isn't enough to just read the bible but we really must know the doctrine as well.

What is striking about my knowledge of the doctrine is the fact that the *knowledge* came as revealed to me by the

Holy Spirit in prayers, and I searched for its validation in the CCC. This has also been the reason why I couldn't be swayed any longer when detractors kept on blaming the priests, or the Roman Catholic Church for brainwashing me, because I know with full certainty that it wasn't the priest nor the church that brainwashed me. I knew of the truth before I heard them spoken or validated to me.

I didn't used to know the doctrine – and for a very long time, I refused to acknowledge it because I rely purely on God's direct and private revelations to me that I get in prayer – but there is a danger to this reliance too - I could get hi-jacked by my spiritual pride, which is significantly detrimental to me if I don't keep myself aware. So, God, made me aware. There was a time – where God would not permit me to hear him. God would even block me from going to the Blessed Sacrament, or to attend Mass even if I really made the effort. And you would wonder, why? Would God really do that? Or the demons? Always remember that "nothing happens without God's permission."

In my case, yes. I was relying purely on the routine – it was purely mechanical for me and I took *pleasure* in simply relying on God speaking directly to my heart thru the discernment I get from the Holy Spirit. One day, he stopped. I was so disturbed. Confused. I was also under attacked – mentally, emotionally, and psychologically. I was doing everything right, as far as I know. But God revealed to me directly as well the necessity for me to know the doctrine. He spelled it literally when I talked to my Spiritual Director, and the ministry of spiritual liberation. Also, since, I love to debate – which very often times function like a double-bladed sword for me *spiritually*, I learned that I simply cannot keep bluffing my way to defending the faith. I have to learn more. God gave me a crash course on Catechism while I was out of body in Vietnam. But it took several years for me to decipher what I literally saw. The communication out of body was non-verbal. It was like watching a silent film yet it was so telepathic. This was how I became more and more confident that the Roman Catholic Church is the authority of God because all the vision I saw while out of body, was succinctly articulated in the Catechism of the Catholic Church. It was truly an "a-ha" moment for me when I started learning about the doctrine.

Christianity is a manifestation of God's great love for us. *"For God so love the world, that he gave his only begotten son, that who so ever believe in him should not perish, but have everlasting life." (John 3:16).* Love can only come from God alone. When one falls in love with God, I guarantee 101%, you will become Catholic, even without prodding. You will become Catholic because you will know what is the "truth" with your *love for God.* This is the key phrase. I dare all of those who belong in other religion to actually claim they are in love with God. To love God is to be like the saints – the willingness to abandon all that doesn't please God for the love of God. We cannot truly love unless we are honest. Honesty is crucial and true love can never manifest in a state of dishonesty. Not the love of religion or leaders, etc. – "Love of God", where one can have that direct experience of personally suffering for God. God will lead you home if you truly love him. Love is the key. Only you will know that. That moment you decide to become Catholic as an adult – only you can discover that and no other. We, Catholics can only pray for you. We can only stand by the truth.

It doesn't sound right to say, we need to defend our Catholic faith in the spiritual realm, but politically, yes it makes sense to do so, due to the policies that will hinder us from defending the truth of God – although before, when my faith was quite immature, this is how I would see it – like a religion that needs defending but no, being Christian under the Authority of the Roman Catholic Church don't need defending. You know why? Because God is in control. But who needs defending? Us. Our humanity. We are so vulnerable to evil because of the offenses caused by our ancestors that unless we decisively commit to cutting them, will continue to infest our society until the end of time. The only arms we need is the Rosary, which is only the Catholic Church will encourage to pray. The seven sacraments that can only be performed by Catholic priests are instituted by no less than Jesus himself. And this is why the Catholic clergy is being attacked because without them, how can we receive the sacrament of baptism to wash away the original sins of Adam & Eve? How can we receive the sacrament of reconciliation so we can be forgiven and be eligible to do reparations for our offenses done to God? How can we protect the future generation if we cannot receive the sacrament of matrimony? How can we die in a state of grace when we are old and demented without the sacrament of anointing? And so on and so forth?

LIFE OSCILLATES

Life is not linear. It oscillates

Life is a journey. The only true judge of your success is you. I learned the hard way that life is not even about being successful. Life is simply about serving a purpose in whichever way you can until we take our last breath. What is important is we live with integrity. Always. I learned that integrity is a person's most powerful lifeline. I know this to be really true from experience. I love looking at myself in the mirror because of this.

One can never prepare enough for life but we can only prepare for death by living each day as our last. We have zero control over our minds or health as we age. Living Life is like art. It's always original. It can't be copied nor completely replicated. For me, my greatest discovery and/or success, that will remain constant and true until the end of my life is finding God and in knowing with absolute certainty that he is real.

This knowledge; this gift of faith is my true north. The catch is, the process of discovery can never be duplicated. It is always uniquely experienced. This discovery also made me realize how eternally blessed I am to be alive. I am so grateful that I had been allowed to live. This gratefulness motivates me to constantly do more with my life. I work and earn so I can serve a purpose. I make goals so I can continually serve a purpose. So just live. Count your blessings. Love yourself no matter what. It's your best friend for life. It is indeed, the greatest love of all. Always find the courage never to compare yourself. Be confident of who you are and your own story. Success is not a one size fits all. It's not acquired by having a title, or a bank account. Find the courage to forgive. The ability to forgive is not for the weak. It's for the strong. It takes courage to forgive.

Speaking as someone who has gone thru several episodes of life-altering trauma, I sincerely wish, if I could turn back time that there was a faster and easier way to understand *forgiveness*. Victor Frankl did emphasize this in his book too, "Man's Search for Meaning" and yet, in the absence of faith, I think forgiveness cannot be truly or fully understood. Forgiveness is not repression. It's the exact opposite. Forgiveness is taking power to accept and letting go of things, memories and events that don't nourish our souls. Yes, anger is a valid emotion and one who has been traumatized should be able to express and feel it - it's true but only to a certain extent that it doesn't hurt another, even if it's valid. Causing hurt to another further delays the healing process. It contaminates even more and solidifies the trauma.

Forgiveness is surrendering to the pain, enduring the pain, accepting the pain - there is no repression here. As what I understand with Frankl, accepting or embracing pain doesn't mean the problems will go away, it means, one's capacity to embrace bigger problems increases. With reason alone, one is being asked to accept the unreasonable. Then what? We are allowed to feel anger, sorrow, grief and talk about it. There was a time I was advised to stop thinking there is a reason for everything so I don't expect and entertain further expectations nor hope, because false hopes cause more hurt. The advice was simply – to go thru it all. Just follow the process. In the process, there is the danger of committing suicide because one feels "no one can understand nor take away one's pain – no one". If there is no reason for the trauma, then what's the point of accepting? A reasonable person will say, "*Fight for yourself because you are worth it.*" But a traumatized person will often say, "*what for?*" Others would say, it's all in your head. Mind over matter. You decide what you want for yourself. Again, there is emphasis on taking control and being strong. So, the person tries and tries again, but it doesn't work.

The person starts to acknowledge, maybe "*I am not worthy to be alive because I am not strong enough to take control of my pain.*" This is often the root cause of depression. The feeling of worthlessness. When we decide that "*no one can ever take away our pain; that there is no one that can help; that there is no one who can really see me and what I feel inside.*" Not many people can get out of this mental and emotional trap once they are already in this state. The key in mental health is how to stop someone from getting into this mental state; But if they are there already? How to get them out of it is like sticking a needle in a haystack. It will require "divine" intervention.

With faith and reason, one understands that the objective of every trauma is to strengthen a person into enduring more pain. In the absence of faith, that is impossible to comprehend because it doesn't mean anything. In the absence of faith, there is no motivation to endure it because no human, as we know of, is worth enduring such pain. Well, in better times, we know ourselves would be worth it – ultimately but when we are traumatized, it is but natural that we often feel worthless, and guilty of shame for allowing such things to happen to us. We would recount the memories in our heads over and over again how we could have changed our decisions so such trauma wouldn't happen to us, and often times, we are met with a big wall of denial and unforgiveness – Unforgiveness towards our own selves.

People mean well when they tell someone to forgive – forgiving oneself is first on the list. Forgiving oneself allows one to accept what happened. Forgiving oneself allows one to accept the reality of the pain. Forgiving oneself allows one to simply surrender to the notion that we are not in control of what happens in our lives and consider the possibility that there is an invisible hand that is leading us into a different path. The decision to accept there is a bigger entity that is in control of our lives requires humility. To determine who is this invisible hand is the lifeline – the crucial part of life and healing because it can go in so many ways. Depending on one's support system or the absence thereof, this identification or determination makes this a critical moment of a traumatized person's life.

Forgiveness is a very powerful tool. It takes a significantly strong person to be able to do this and people in trauma, should aspire to have this strength to forgive because it is the only way to liberate oneself. Without which, we may be able to move on, do great things, do big things, but one will always remain vulnerable to the trauma of the past unless one forgives. Forgiveness is key to healing. I really don't know of any another way

Another important gift God has given man is, our propensity to make mistakes. Dare to fail! Failure is not for the weak. It's for the strong. Failure builds character, if you learn from it. Failure inspires humility. Be humble while remaining confident. Maintaining the balance is not for the weak. It takes strength to maintain restraint from falling into vanity. Humility gives one strength to forgive. It is critical for a person to come up with a tool to remember how to forgive ourselves, not only others.

Another critical virtue to acquire is to be kind. Kindness is not for the weak. It takes courage to be kind. Kindness fuels your ability to forgive. Every day we are alive is an opportunity for redemption. While it is true that Christ's death was our salvation but the caveat is, *"it is only if we choose to live like him."* **Choose** is the buzzword. To choose to be like him is to be willing to be crucified because of love, mercy and compassion. We were all designed to be good. We are all good. I completely understood this but somehow, we are all prone to deceptions of the evil one. It is so easy to forget that we are all innately designed to be good.

It is so easy to be distracted. I am guilty of this – All the time, every minute - no, seconds. Regardless, we still carry that obligation to close our open doors and make the choice to follow Christ. There is no excuse. There is no other way. It is not about religion at all nor about politics but the specific virtues that Jesus Christ demonstrated from birth to death and ultimately, his resurrection. The question is: *Why do we need to preach? Why, as a follower of Christ, are we oblige to share God's goodness?*

Isn't it enough to just individually save ourselves? We now go back to the caveat of living like Christ. Jesus Christ demonstrated how it is done and that it can be done. Remember "for God so love the world that he gave is only begotten son"?

It's never been an "I" thing but a "We" thing. To be like Christ is to love all! Love – so easy to talk about, so easy to conceive, so easy to imagine but to truly "love" requires significant divine strength. Every day is our reset button. We don't know how many tomorrows we have left in this lifetime so it is best to spend each day with care and a firm commitment to live like Christ.

EVENING SUNSHINE

Bright darkened sky,
Hope-filled dilemma
Sweet painful love
Daylight in the Eve...
Contrasting emotions
Of deceitful truths
As harmonious chaos
Sees beauty in ugliness
Ques of answers
Belief in doubts
View the nonexistence
Of the evening sunshine

S omewhere along the way, while gazing at my Facebook page, I came up with a profound realization that although knowledge and technology continue to advance exponentially towards the Nth dimension, humanity in general still see reality in 3D, and it has nothing to do with how intelligent one can be. Human psychology is indeed one hard nut to crack. People just communicate differently. Secrets are anathema to freedom and democracy.

So does privacy and censorship. Finding the skill to deal with freedom is still an unpopular quest but I'm quite certain it will become a trend eventually as social media platforms like Facebook continue to grow like mushrooms. What Facebook has provided the world is the opportunity to be free – to be liberated from the shackles of social exclusivity. If one gets fired for it, oh well– perhaps it's an opportunity for one to pursue something one will never get fired for and that is to discover the skill to deal with freedom. In my case, Facebook has allowed me to document impromptu quotes borne from a passionately deep moment, where otherwise, it could have been left unsaid, unharnessed.

> *Is "human love" (like faith and religion) too irrational or "too naive" to be considered a key factor in solving the world's problems? If "Hitler" had fallen in love like Ferdinand Marcos for Imelda, do you think there would be a gas chamber?*[1]

I used to recall someone from my research methods class pursuing a study on "why do people get their hearts broken and correlate it on how it affects their dating methods". My professor, a clinical psychologist, didn't seem to appear surprised or taken aback by what seemed to be a rather "trivial" question or let's just say, downright personal topic. He, in fact, acknowledged the proponent's proposal as a rather reasonable topic, and proceeded on discussing possible indicators that the proponent came up with. Is that compassion or what?

---

1   Ferdinand & Imelda Marcos was the President and First Lady, respectively of The Philippines from 1965-1986.

Based on my observations or perhaps my personal experience, I noticed that people often correlate one's personal breakdown or success to a significant other. There are many lines that goes, "Behind every successful man, there's a woman" or "the secret to a successful life is in finding the right partner", otherwise, it's the recipe for a miserable life.

There are many books on love and relationships, and I think I've read so many of them. I pretty much followed most of the rule books out there on dating. I'm pretty confident I did most of it right. But why is Mr. Right still elusive? I'll get back to this later.

I think, the thing that makes "falling in love" so destructive for many is not because we met the wrong person or met someone at the wrong time but because we subconsciously desire a certain person reflecting how we feel at a certain time. The problem is timing. Timing of course accounts for luck. Timing becomes a problem when one is not equipped with the right batteries.

The batteries would mean, emotional wisdom. I used to recall a homily back in my high school years by the president of our university, the late Fr. Roderick Salazar, SVD. My memory of the details is a little fuzzy but the story somewhat goes a little like this. There was once a man who met a watch inventor in an airport. The watch inventor was explaining to this man that his watch has the capacity to transport him into another time. His watch could also predict what will happen in the next minute, hour or future. He even demonstrated to him what will happen in the next minute and true enough, the watch worked! The man was so impressed that he begged to trade his humble Rolex watch. The inventor agreed. As the man was about to leave, the inventor called him back and said, "Wait! You are forgetting two things!" The man turned around and check on his belongings and wondered what it was that he forgot. The inventor turned and pointed at the two oversized suit cases. The man said, "that's not mine; mine is right here". The inventor smiled and said, "I know. These suitcases are for your watch. They are your batteries. Without them, your watch won't work".

Fr. Salazar explained that in life, we need two big batteries, *"Scientia et Virtus"* Science and Virtues. Without which, we won't go very far in life. We won't be able to achieve great things without both.

Similarly in finding the right partner. Often times, we seek for our batteries from our partner, which in and of itself is already flawed, and for lack of a better term, wrong. In observing successful marriages of great couples in history, both couples are great in their own right. Of course, since we don't really know what happens in a marriage. On a small side note, and subject to another argument and analysis, success is never without pain or trials, success isn't limited to time. When two great people marry, it is their work and achievement that extend off of them, not their relationships. It is their individual contribution to humanity and not the details that happen within their married life.

I noticed, that if we dissect each of their backgrounds, each of them is equipped with their own sets of batteries. They do not draw energy from each other. They unite their batteries together creating enough energy surplus to help them propel through life together without getting drained. The batteries they both carry are not duplicates of each other but are the right match. This means, their values match as their interests match.

When we are young, we are often misled by romantic novelists that love "just happens"; that love is simply beyond reason. At a certain point, I believe this. But the question is, is love a feeling or a fact to be discovered outside of one self or from another person or is that love already within us waiting to be realized?

My answer would be both. I think one who hasn't fully realized the love already within that person cannot find love outside of oneself. Mr. Right or Mrs. Right is not a missing piece as most romantics would claim it to be, "you complete me." Mr. Right and Mrs. Right are merely bonuses or in business terms, dividends.

Human beings are a bunch of energy magnets. Every day we use up energy. Hence, we need to constantly charge our batteries. When we are alone, it is harder to do so many things without getting drained, that is why we often need the support of friends or family to draw energy support from when our own stack run out.

But friends and family also need that energy and have to multiply those energy to several other people too. This means that we can only use what they are willing or capable to share at a certain time. We can't expect them to always have significant supply of energy at all times.

The advantage of having a partner is that, you are in synced. Your batteries are in synced and if anyone needs some power up, you have enough energy surplus to give to others without draining yours. The couple that has enough realized love for themselves know when enough is enough. They know when to draw the line where their love for themselves and for each other are in peril. They then know when to hold back. They both know when to protect themselves from getting drained.

So why is Mr. Right so elusive for me knowing what I know? Is knowing enough? In the two big batteries I mentioned above, it would seem that the knowing pertains to the Science aspect in life. But what about virtues? Virtue? Virtue is a whole lot different. Virtue is the instinctive and subconscious aspect of the self. It's often times referred to as the "unknown", or the God-factor.

Most intellectuals have managed to convince themselves that the God-factor doesn't exist. Hence, the justification for the none-existence of the *one* or Mr. Right. Many of these intellectuals jump from one partner to another where they can draw energy from. The modern-day definition of this particular type would be, emotional vampires. The more they do that, the more their virtues battery drains because the virtue battery requires a lot of restraint. The virtues battery is like art. It grows when we give enough of ourselves.

Finding Mr. Right or Mrs. Right would seem like a gift. A stroke of luck. And luck often correlates to the God-factor. The *one* is a reward. When we store up enough good virtues in our battery bank, the likelihood of finding the "one" becomes higher, why? How many in this world do you think is able to grow their virtues battery bank while fattening their science bank? I don't think not many. How many of them actually grows it at the same time and meet? Voila! There goes the one.

On the reversal, happy are those who do not need to store their Science bank. Again, only very few are gifted with a fat virtues bank that they don't need to grow their Science.

Sometimes, some people are able to re-charge enough batteries for both in their lifetime enough to enjoy it while they live. Most often, others are often just half-way there when they are already in their death beds. The polarity of the Evening Sunshine is actually not that wide if you come to think of it. It can be slim if one is just strong enough to store both batteries together without draining one or the other.

UNDERSTANDING MYSELF

I have been in relationships where I have given enough of myself to a point that I allowed myself to lose faith in a divine being. And that is serious because my faith is fundamental to who I am as a human being. And that is also the worst decision I made in my life. Once you lose that, one loses clarity. One loses that grace of knowing. Much of that choice was not because I was being selfless but because I was insecure and impatient – impatient to understand what God's plan for me was because I was jealous of what other women my age had at that time. I was so afraid to be left behind and to be pitied upon. It was pride, in all totality that caused me to open myself to another person. My intention was already flawed to begin with. My heart was incapable to give and accept love even when mentally I was willing myself to do so because my underlying motivation was driven by pride.

I have allowed myself to believe in what my so-called partner or companion believed in, or lack thereof so that I can feel good enough for that person. I have allowed myself to be stupid – to act stupid, to not think and be this heart-struck girl with moony eyes. I have allowed myself to cry over men. I have allowed myself to really surrender to a point of utter silliness. I have allowed myself to be compared to other women and I have allowed myself to be subjected to emotional humiliation. Yes, I know how to be a girl. I know how to be that kind of girl. I have been there, done that. I have quite a handful of stories to tell in that department. In so doing, I almost destroyed my self-esteem. I tried so hard to be that kind of girl everybody expects me to be thinking that I will find happiness there. But what did happen, and I don't regret doing all of the above for one moment, is I allowed myself to be lost completely. In so doing, I found myself completely, as well.

I always wanted– No, *desired* to love and be loved. I was so hungry for it. Hungry would be an understatement. I was starving for it. My friends and cousins would tease me that I fall in love crazy. And that it takes me a long time to get over someone. And to some extent, it's really true. Why? Because I always only wanted <u>one</u> person. Just one. Not two or three. Just one. I didn't want to have a boyfriend just because. I even refused to acknowledge my other relationships as so because I am committed to just have one. I indeed acknowledged just one, and that one official relationship couldn't be more platonic than my non-official relationships.

I acknowledge one puberty love at 19 (I am a super late bloomer) where I cried heaps. I acknowledge one romanticized love at 21 driven primarily by pride and insecurity. And one totally unexpected, great love that I never saw coming – A love that scares most people away. A love that helped me found the courage to face my own horrors and deal with my own brokenness. This was something I considered a divine gift. I grew up... Finally. And the last one was a Love that led me to learn about "Sacred Love" – a love that transforms, a love that understand, a love that endures, a love that sacrifice, and a love that desire to save one's soul. This last love – led me to realize how I have fallen in love with God. If I had not known of this kind of love, I wouldn't have recognized the love I feel for God. I never learned of love growing up – I didn't know how to truly give it that's why I never knew how it felt to love. God had to teach me. God had to let me go thru several phases of love so that I could recognize the love I feel for him.

I've always known, deep down, what I want in order to be truly happy with someone and my subconscious self knew I was lying to myself. In order to justify my wrong decisions, I used to overcompensate my mistakes by making my feelings and experience to be more than just the experience. I tend to put the guy/s on a pedestal after the non-relationship relationship ends so that I'd at least feel that all my non-relationship relationships were meaningful. I refused to start something new by hanging on to the previous non-relationship relationships because I really don't want to make another mistake. I was broken inside. I knew I was already broken before I started to desire for a relationship.

I realized eventually that the secret to joy is right inside of me. I must have the courage to accept me first. I have to be me. I have to have the freedom to be who I really am without having to apologize for it. In the same way, I have to be willing to accept the other for all that he is without him having to apologize for it. And for this reason, timing does really matter. I have met plenty of wonderful, wonderful men in my life. Beautiful men. This is me looking on hindsight. Except, when I met those men, I was with someone else. When my emotions are already attached to someone, I'd have to wait until it dies down before I can consider another person. This is what I used to be. I was so dependent on my feelings and not by faith. While I used to be self-righteous on being a committed person, I was still driven primarily by feelings, which is ultimately very flawed.

When I met those men, I didn't realize I was without faith and because I was without faith, I couldn't see their beauty. Because I was without faith, I couldn't see them. When I did, I was already too late. They came not once but more often than I thought. I was stuck looking at my closed doors for so long because of my lack of clarity that when I did see the open doors, I was too late. But is it fair to blame myself? I'd say no. I'd say, it was not meant for me. That's where the God factor comes in. How can I possibly know my way if I was lost to begin with? The only thing I know I was guilty of is my faith wasn't strong enough and it wasn't because I was selfish and unwilling to be with someone.

During those times that I was yearning to be with someone, even when I was moving on a snail pace compared to other women, I took so long to be with another because I needed time to repair what is broken in me. Somehow, I had the wisdom to be aware of it. What good am I for anyone if I am broken inside?

So what does being me mean? I am opinionated. I am deep and shallow at the same time. To such extreme. I may be funny and utterly serious at the same time. Why? That's how my personal history shaped the person that I am today. I have no control over my childhood. I have no control over my childhood decisions but I know I do have control over my adult decisions. Having said that, while our childhood experiences and decisions can be altered by how we choose to interpret it now, as an adult, still in a lot of ways, our childhood still shape the behavior we have as an adult. We can alter the negative interpretations but we cannot completely alter our innate and inherent traits – our predisposition.

I am predisposed to be high strung. Some people are able to quell it but eventually, later in life, it will still come out. At least I have the wisdom to understand that. Having the wisdom to know myself, the things I don't want and can't live with or without, and understanding my responsibilities to the other, wouldn't you want to be with someone just like that as well? Knowing what a good gamble can do to one's life, the risks they entail, the extent of damage a failed relationship can do to a person, would one still be careless about it? I would think not. Having said that, my not being careless does not mean I was or am unwilling to be with someone.

I am willing except I am quite happy with my freedom or so I thought. I convinced myself that I am happy even when I am alone. I hadn't even tried feeling joy when I was with someone. I have even reached a point to ask; do I really need to have a husband? The thought of having one was something I can't imagine yet at that time. If I can deal with my being single, then that's all that really matters in the end, right? At the end of the day, we are always on our own even with a husband or a partner. When we face the mirror, we are first and foremost, an individual. And even without a partner or companion, we should be confident to feel joy even when we are alone. Shouldn't we?

My only hesitation to staying single back then was my overwhelming desire for motherhood, which only manifested after my NDE/OBE in Vietnam. Though I do not care so much about public opinion on being a single mother at that time but I do worry about the longevity of my life, how much I have left in it or how much time I have before I lose my memory or the consciousness to guide my future kids.

I have been stalking the Danish guy for the longest time. My lack of closure with him prevented me from finding someone new. Men always fall short compared to him. He was, by far, the highest benchmark. Except for one thing, he wasn't Catholic. He was borne from a multi-divorced family. His father was divorced from another family and his mother was divorced from another family. He was born in between. My instincts were still correct why I didn't take a chance with him – it was the most that I could handle. If I went any further, understanding my brokenness, I would not have survived. We would not have survived because he too, was quite broken. But loving him was instrumental in my transformation.

In 2014, I couldn't take it anymore. I missed him so much I felt like I was going to die. I was not being melodramatic but the feeling was quite accurate. It's like drowning. It was extremely haunting. I messaged him that I am planning to attend a documentary film festival in Copenhagen, and I am hoping to stay with him. I messaged him out of the blue. He was always so kind and welcomed me immediately.

He was so excited that he followed up with me when I will go. Unfortunately, Yolanda happened. I chickened out. I couldn't possibly go to Copenhagen when all of this calamity was happening in my country. But if I truly loved him, who cares about this calamity right? It simply meant; I didn't love him enough the way I thought I was.

I allowed myself to feel afraid, and entertained anxiety, that later turned into pride again. When I replied that I cannot go because of the typhoon and all, he graciously accepted it. I sent him another message thanking him for his hospitability and generosity, but since that time he never read it anymore. It remained unread until I messaged him again in 2018. I found out a year after that he had a girlfriend already, Danish like him. She was different than most of her girlfriends. She was quite simple – unlike the women he was dating before. I had this nagging feeling – this was going to be serious. Before the girl, he had a relationship with an Italian ballerina. I even messaged him about it at how beautiful her girlfriend was. But they broke up shortly after.

In 2016, I was so overweight. I am specially mentioning my being overweight to give context on my mental state. I have always been skinny and I never had to worry about looking big but once I did, it significantly affects my level of confidence and it added up to my insecurities. One day, I stalked the Danish guy again and I found out that he was going to have a baby with his Danish girlfriend. I was devastated. It's like – finally, it's over for me. It is definitely game over. I tore up the letter he gave me at I-House. I tore up our photos that I printed out that I kept on looking on literally every day since 2005.

In my pain, I decided to do something drastic – I joined a triathlon race with less than two months to prepare. I lost so much weight in less than 2 months. I got addicted to training – and in fact, I thought I was falling in love with my coach. Prior to that, I was already praying to God to give me someone – just anyone! I even prayed for God to take away my superficial eyes because I am so picky. I keep on comparing every man I meet to the Danish guy, which cannot be compared because he was just too beautiful, inside & out. I was putting him on a pedestal. But there was nothing more I could do about him. He was going to be a father then.

So, I was hanging on my coach for dear life. Nothing happened between me and my coach – it was all about triathlon training, although what we had was almost like a relationship. It was very personal. He was also previously married and was living with a previously married woman. When I thought I had feelings for him, I didn't realize he had a girlfriend. That was the first time, in my life, that I could understand how it felt to be a mistress. Though I was far from being a mistress but because I was so caught off-guard with my emotions and attachment, even though I knew he had a girlfriend, I was not willing to let go of him.

Again, we never had any romantic relationship. It was purely coaching relationship. As far as we both know, it was just a coaching relationship. But I would get jealous when he was with his girlfriend. There was even a time that his girlfriend got so jealous of me that she eventually attacked me on social media. That was not my finest moment. God let me experience how it was to be on the shoes of another woman – which I am normally so critical and judgmental against.

Gradually, starting in 2016 – my mom's demeanor with me has gotten so much worse. She started attacking me more and more. My brothers used to tiptoe around me because they knew how close I am to our dad and they usually go thru me when they needed help to talk to my father. But one day, because my mom was becoming impossible, my 2nd elder brother tried to pacify me but also because he wanted me to talk to dad about something. They weren't aware yet how in love my father was to my mom until I told them. I told them the best way to go to dad is thru mommy. Anything mommy wants Dad will give. That was the beginning of the end for me. Since that time, I was taken for granted by everyone, literally, save for my dad. My mom grew more powerful in the family. Did I mention I didn't have a job? My dad was giving me $1000 each month to pay for my student loan and I also use it to roll my credit card. I never really saved anything. I didn't really care much about money because I was simply existing.

I have never been attached to money and I always relied on my father's provision which my mom and siblings have grown allergic to. Admittedly, in that aspect, I was very complacent. I was already an Architect. I prided myself into thinking that I didn't need to play the game of the rat race and I didn't want to start needing money. At that time, the possibility that my siblings will turn against me in the way they did to me eventually was not something I could ever imagine in my life. Yes, we always fought since we were little but I always believed they loved me. I was closest to my 2nd elder brother who always motivated me to strive for more in my life, and I was also the one who motivated him to fight when he wanted to give up in his life when his first wife left him. I reminded him who he was and what he was always capable of doing. I remember challenging him and giving it my all, as if my life depended on it. I loved my brothers. I loved my sister.

Even when my eldest brother who was always cruel to me for as long as I can remember, and even when I visited him in Toronto, left me in a restaurant, just because we argued about "fire protection" where he grew so defensive and wanted me to recognize his expertise in the matter, to which it irritated me so much I continued to negate him. He ended up leaving me in a restaurant in the middle of winter just because of that argument. It was trivial but it was such a big deal for him that he left me there. I ended up staying in a hotel, cut short my trip and went back to New York.

Even when my sister also did the same thing to me when I traveled to New York back in 2003, and she got mad with my plans to study in New York City. She literally humiliated me and talked about me never ever going to find a man who will ever take me seriously. It sounded so much like a curse. She asked me to leave her house so I was forced to stay with an old college friend in the city for the remainder of the duration of my trip.

And lastly, even when my 2nd elder brother also locked me out of his apartment where the only available toilet was available the first time, I reviewed for the architecture board exam, which I failed to take because the teller who processed our application at the Philippine Regulatory Commission (PRC) didn't process our application to take the board exam. I got so mad at my brother, we fought and literally asked me to leave his house. I ended up staying with my friend who was reviewing with me.

However, in spite all of that, we have always recovered. I have gotten used to that kind of conflict within the family. It was normal already. We used to have a family group chat where we would always fight, it's always me against them. In fact, during my birthday in 2016, and my sister came to visit from New York, so they wanted to celebrate it in Boracay. It was so timely that I was able to book my mom's timeshare account in Boracay for my birthday. I stayed in my hotel, alone with my helper. I had dinner with them but they were already casting me out like I was an outsider. I think my being "fat" was more of the reason that they didn't want me around — no matter how shallow it may seem but it really affected them because they bullied me about it that entire dinner. I remembered my nieces wanting to spend time with me but then my mom forbade it. Until time came that all of them wouldn't come to me anymore.

But when I started doing triathlon, I got a lot of visibility from Rotary — because I really lost a lot of weight and since triathlon was such a very painful and difficult sport, it was such a big deal that I am able to do it. My nieces started to reach out to me again because they were fascinated by me.

I registered for Vietnam because I wanted to make advances to my coach, admittedly. I was already very conflicted because I have grown so attached to him but I also know that he was a married man (because his marriage wasn't annulled yet). I couldn't understand why I seem to be losing control with myself when I am supposed to be getting closer to God. I was already religious at this time — well, not as religious as I am now but I was already committed to growing my faith. The problem with my efforts at that time was, it was all about me. I had to be faithful to God because

I was afraid of the darkness. I had no concept of love yet. I had no concept of my responsibility as a Christian yet. Oh, I was so far away from that thought process. I was still looking at everything from a very selfish, shallow, and self-entitled human being's point of view.

The entire time I was training and, in each race, I was always praying the Rosary. I would repeat all four mysteries more than 4 times per day, that's like 2,000 Hail Mary's coupled with physical pain. I didn't know anything about reparation but somehow, by the grace of the Holy Spirit, I was already offering it for the conversion of my parents, the Danish guy, and my future husband, whoever he may be. I was very specific with my prayer to God that I hope the next man I will fall in love, it will be the one. I am willing to wait but I want him to be the one. There was a time that I grew impatient and I said to God, "Lord, please give me an assurance that he is around. If he is not yet ready, at least please let me take a peek of him. Just an assurance that I have something to wait for." Many did say that my prayers needed to be specific. It is also important to note that I had always been in doubt on the authenticity of my faith. I asked the Lord, to give me confirmation if my faith in him was authentic. I said it would be a pity that I am making all these efforts only to realize that when I'm dead, I was just lying all along. God surely answered me, while I was Out of Body.

So, when we arrived in Vietnam, I was so infested with the spirit of lust that on the day of the race, I was already planning what I was going to do as soon as I finished the race. Then I died. I didn't expect that at all. Never in my wildest dreams did I ever consider the possibility that I could die. But after I woke up from that 4 to 5 hour *Out of Body* trip, the feelings I had for my coach was completely gone. It's like totally- 200% gone. I was completely liberated from him that I didn't even want to maintain any associations with him.

When I got back to my training crew, the boys who were with me in Vietnam, and notice my interaction with my coach, started teasing me. Since I didn't want them to continue pursuing that direction, I decided to use my Ace card – the Danish guy. I started telling them about my old love story with the Danish guy. That was the only reason why I brought him up again. While I was so proud to show them his picture from his FB, they clicked "add friend"– I was so shocked. The Danish guy unfriended me somewhere along the way. Even though I was shocked, but I always trusted him to be very rational, and since we haven't really talked or communicated since 2014, I was confident he will add me. He didn't only not add me, he also removed the option of me adding him. I was surprised to have that kind of reaction from him. And that started to bother me in a good way, on the possibility that he could still be affected by me that he wouldn't even consider the possibility of adding me.

When I travelled with another Rotarian friend, also named Cathy, I told her my story with the Danish guy. She dared me to come clean with him once and for all. I told her my desire to become a mom and I needed a sperm donor. At that time, I still didn't have *any* understanding of the doctrine of the Roman Catholic Church – zero. I still maintained a disobedient thought process. I really wanted a baby from the Danish guy. So, she suggested to test the waters and see if he was already married and if not, I will go in for the kill. Since I didn't know how to make him respond, my friend suggested that I will message him as if I am in trouble and that if he truly cared for me, he will respond.

I told him I need to tell him something important and if he would be so kind, to let me know when it would be okay to call him. Exactly as how my friend suspected, he replied. He messaged me immediately to ask if everything's is okay with me. He was really worried and told me to call him anytime. So, I gave him a call immediately. I found out that he wasn't married so right there and then, I told him that I couldn't think of another man I want to father my child, and if he would be willing to be my sperm donor. I wasn't contented with that, I added, "you don't need to decide now. Maybe it's something you may want to discuss with your girlfriend. You can trust I am not looking to get married; I just want to have a child and I want it done the natural way." He was absolutely so kind about it, and told me how flattered he was that I asked him, of all people. He was actually laughing. He asked me to wait at least two weeks and he will get back to me. He seemed excited. I was so excited. The following day, I went to an obstetrician to check my labs. I was already imagining having a baby with him. Then later that evening, my phone rang. I started to feel scared because it's far from two weeks. We just spoke yesterday. It was him. He told me, he has made his decision. He phrased it in this manner, "I spoke with my girlfriend and she has grown possessive with my sperm. Had you asked me before, it would have been different".

This really broke me. I wasn't only broken by the idea of not having him but I was much more broken by the idea that I wouldn't become a mother. I was so looking forward to the "blue eyed" baby. I ended up telling him all the things

I never got to tell him. All the time I kept the truth from him, and the lie that I never wanted to get married too. I told him honestly how I felt. Then he blocked me. I was finally able to move on from him after that.

I focused my attention on training. I let my nieces train with me until such time that my brother's eldest daughter started to disobey me over a boy in my running team, and dared me that she was already an adult, and she insisted she can do whatever she wants. At that time, I was still quite controlling but what really irked me was the disobedience being their aunt, who cared for them when they were little. The disrespect didn't sit well with me and I got so angry. To make things worse, my nieces knew how much power they have over me when it comes to my dad. They know that they have more edge if I am the one who is angry. Since they were hiding behind my dad, I was literally prevented from entering our building. I was banned, for the first time.

I was so angry with my father then. I felt so betrayed because I thought, I am after all his own daughter yet he would favor my nieces more. What I failed to realize then was, what my father was against with was not exactly me, but my behavior. It didn't matter that I was his favorite or that he loved me, but he will not let me abuse my nieces just because I am his daughter. My father was right in every aspect but I couldn't see it at that time. I kept on pushing everyone to a point that when the time came that I was truly being righteous, I have already lost my authority. I was much too late and I didn't even see it coming.

Going back to our tax bureau, our family business was significantly hemorrhaging money. No matter what we do, the financial loses kept in coming because of our back taxes that we are paying by the millions. It didn't help that my father is financing a very huge land in Leyte to keep armed squatters from coming in. We were losing money. My brothers, this time were bailing my father out but they still get it back anyways, double than what they let him borrow. It is important to note that all of my brothers' businesses were formed because of my father. They never paid my dad a single royalty, never paid rent, and also absorbed some of my father's workers. I could feel the hurt and disappointment my father felt towards my siblings but not once did my father ever condoned me fighting back at them.

I initially thought my brothers needed a scape goat to blame because both of them were already planning to shut down my father's business. My father tried to hand both of them the reigns in the business but due to different management culture, many of my father's workers would quit because of them. So, because of my financial problems and excessive fights with my sister, my brothers set me up to work for the family business again, and I was in charge of marketing. I felt they totally underestimated my capacity to close a sale. They initially thought that giving me that role, will lead to the eventual closure of the business because I won't be able to get new projects.

However, as soon as I got back to work, I was able to close more than ten projects. And to top it all, there was another project that my eldest brother decided to drop. As we were nearing the bid deadline, he still wasn't willing to do something about it. He did manage to get us to the final bidding stage when he decided to quit. Since he had lost interest, I decided to take over. I signed off on all the bid documents, and by God's grace, we were selected as the final candidates. The other bidders were from Manila, and we were the only ones from Cebu. I flew to Manila just to close this deal.

At that time, my eldest brother was all too willing to skin me alive because he got mad that I continued the bidding and I signed off on the bid documents. He got even more mad because he didn't want me to get the credit and was telling my mother that I stole it from him. Everybody in the office knew that he has already abandoned it. But the three of us, went to Manila. Truth be told, it was my strategy that closed the deal. I know the total contract amount and the substitutions they made that affected the overall costing, so I know that if I give a seven Million discount, which was supposedly my commission, I could still get it based on their substitutions and approval not to import a product that we also manufacture ourselves, using our own brand.

I happen to be the Quality Management Representative (QMR) of our manufacturing department, a position I held since 2001. Nobody has ever paid attention to this department because my father has only been using these products as added incentives to clients. We were never really earning from it. But yes, it was my boldness, confidence and professional approach to the client that made them closed the deal. I was aware of my influence and my capacity to communicate, especially with their type of clientele. My brothers have a different strategy – a more local, Cebuano approach but these clients were from Manila. My 2nd elder brother's closer was not him, it was his 2nd wife, which was not part of the entourage. My brothers knew, I closed that deal. But right after that, my 2nd brother was growing more agitated the more I got involved in operations. I was trying to tie up the loose ends, while they seem adamant to keep it bleeding. Until at such point, I had to take drastic measures in protecting my interest by asking my father to sign off certain documents to me. My brothers got so angry, & my mom got angry as well. It was dangerous when it's my mom who gets angry because my father cannot protect me anymore. After their golden wedding, my mom already held all the power. She would humiliate my dad in public and my father will just endure it. It was like my father was atoning for all the offenses he caused my mother.

FINDING LOVE, AGAIN

I am resigned to trust that God has a divine plan for me. If God wills it; he wills it. There's only one Architect of my life. In God I trust. And then I met the late Monsignor Fred Kreikenbeek in 2019. So, what exactly happened after meeting the late Monsignor? Before I go there, let me walk you through on what happened before meeting Monsignor.

In early 2019, while my conflict with my family was peaking, I got visited by my friend from Nepal – which was truly a welcome break for me. We decided to go diving in Siquijor because one of my cousins just gave me a new project in one of his food chain branches. Going there, I never felt so alone because my entire family was against me. I started yearning for someone. So, when I went to Siquijor, I wanted my friend to try a discovery dive and while looking for the dive master, I met this French man – somehow, when I met him – it's like the world stopped. After my friend's dive, we decided to stay another night so we could dive again the following day just so I could spend more time with him. Unfortunately, we didn't he was quite distant. But because of my sheer desperation in my family, I didn't want to let go of the idea of him. My Nepalese friend was really encouraging me. A few months after, I was so motivated to train for the next triathlon race but more motivated because of the French guy. I brought my entire training crew to Siquijor so I can be with the French diver whom I have been texting while in Cebu. He knew my intentions of going to Siquijor. I have never ever thrown myself so boldly to any guy until that time. I was that desperate. But the French man literally turned me down. Flat out, no. He refused to show up where we agreed to meet and didn't reply at all.

When we got back to Cebu, my father called me and got so mad at me because why did I betray him in opening a new bank account. I told my father that my brother said he already knew. I got so mad with my brother for going behind my dad's back. I got mad at my mom for betraying my dad and even forging my signature, being one of the shareholders.

This was the beginning of the end of all ends. I confronted them over chat. I was very confident that it will just be one of those fights where we will always recover. The possibility of them casting me out of the family was not something I even considered for a moment. But they surely did.

While all the family conflicts were happening, I was diverting my thoughts by going diving – trying to catch the French man's attention. I was literally so desperate. It's like I had nowhere to run. I was communicating with God the entire time but I wasn't truly that pious yet. I still pray daily while training but the rest of the time, I allowed myself to get distracted with worldly things. But the Vietnam incident was always more than enough to keep my focus back to

God. I prayed to God to give me a chance to show someone that I know how to love. Because in all the time I thought I was in love, I have never actually expressed it to anyone. Not even to Simone. I wasn't sure any more if I really know how to love. I was very hungry. I just need to be able to love someone, more than me being loved. I thought if I don't know how to love, how can I learn to recognize that I am being loved? I needed to love someone, with all of my heart. I never knew I could need anything so bad. I needed it more than I wanted to breathe.

I got into a scandal among the Scuba community. I got criticized for my so-called "reckless scuba-diving" behavior. I would dive so deep and I get scolded that I am making scuba diving in the Philippines dangerous. I was encouraged to learn scuba diving again.

At the amount of scandal I was getting, I was dead set on finding me the most reliable scuba diving instructor ever, whose diving instruction reputation was highly respected to be the safest. Then I found him. His reputation preceded him that he was strict and firm. As for me, I never really took scuba diving seriously. It's just a hobby for me, and the only reason why I got interested in it again was because of the French guy. I was just trying to catch his attention. But since I have gone in so deep with the scuba community, I started to get affected by all their criticisms. But since I still have a triathlon race to finish, I had to wait until that race was over, which I finished and completed, successfully.

The first time I saw my instructor, he was with two women with him. He was not typically my type and if not for my coach who already broke my standards, I probably wouldn't look. But for some reason, he had a presence that made me want to look. I was waiting for him to turn around so I can initiate a conversation with him but he never did. It was only much later, when the pressure from the scuba community have finally gotten to me that I decided to call him. The first time I saw him, I was late. He was really strict. I was curious if he was married so I tried to scoop it out of him just from curiosity and he laughed like it was such a ridiculous question. We always shared a witty banter even if I don't try. He seems to laugh at my responses. I really didn't mind it.

After the Ironman 70.3-mile race, as I was looking at my feeds, I saw the page of an old high school classmate, who was specializing in kitchen installation. I was curious so I thought I'll touch base with her. At that time, Monsignor Kreikenbeek was already working with her – helping her process her family. I wanted so much to meet Monsignor for the longest time. So, one day, I finally did. I was finally able to make a proper confession and he anointed me. Monsignor made me recite the Consecration to the Sacred Heart of Jesus and the Blessed Virgin, and I remember making a vow of chastity.

After that, I talked to my old classmate how I want to be married and later, I can enter the convent but I really needed to be a mother first. She encouraged me to at least start somewhere like dating someone. I said, my only options are overseas. And she insisted it has to be local once and for all, and at least try to have a relationship with someone that I actually get to see in person. She encouraged me to start searching from my phonebook.

My scuba instructor was quite flirty in his text, and there were even times I would feel taken aback at how fresh he seemed. Later, I found out he was always like that to every student, male or female. So, when I checked my phone, it was only his text that stood out. My old classmate said, why don't you start with him? And so, I did. I followed his lead and we started texting.

The night before I was going to hear an early morning mass in Theotokos Shrine in Carcar city, southern Cebu, where Monsignor will be celebrating, he texted me if I would be interested to join him for a dive. I told him, "Sure after I hear mass in Carcar". Then he texted me back, asking me if I hear mass daily. I told him I try my best to hear mass as often as I can. When I went to join him to dive, I found him to be very funny. Unlike the first time I met him, where he seemed to be irritated with me for being late. That evening, I was feeling lonely, and thought, maybe I'll invite him out to dinner. And so, I did. I forgot his reply – I don't think he replied. But I remember, we were having so much fun with divers from Hong Kong. Then he started texting me incessantly the entire time we were driving. The following day, I showed my helper a photo of us together, and she thought we looked great. And so, I started entertaining the possibility that something could come of this. We started to dive regularly. He was always hot and cold with me.

He would be strict at first, then he would make me laugh. As the day went by, I grew to like him a lot. I respected him. I learned he used to be the chief editor of a national newspaper in the Philippines but US edition. I learned he graduated from a university I failed to get accepted from in college. I was completely surprised. It humbled me. That was precisely his entire effect on me – he kept humbling me down and I was all too willing to be humbled. I was afraid of him – of disappointing him.

He was a very reserved man even if he can be really funny and sociable. I noticed he wanted to get rid of me very early on – he threatened to return my money and asked me to look for another instructor elsewhere because he thought I was very stubborn – which I didn't understand why. In my mind, I was already in my humblest- how was I stubborn? Then he asked me to drop home two of his students, one was a retiree and used to work for NASA. I ended up telling him about my life. I don't know if they talked but the following day, just when I thought my instructor has kicked me out of his program, he messaged me to go on another dive and so I did. While on the boat, he insisted I will finally pass his exam so I can move on from it and we can focus on diving. I was so confused why I keep on failing the dive table exam. Being with him made me so nervous that I felt so pressured not to disappoint him. That has never ever happened in my life. I just couldn't think straight with him around.

He told me to pick a place where I can take my exam, so I picked a place across my church. It felt like a date but he refused to order anything. He then told me if he can hear mass while I finish my exam. I looked sad but then he asked me if I wanted to join him for mass instead. I considered that as our very first real date – inside the church. He was very charming. He also had a very nice voice when he sings. A voice in my head suggested something and I asked the Lord, is he the one? After mass, I took the exam but then it was cut short because he learned that his good friend just died. He asked me to drop him off somewhere. I didn't know what to say to him to make him feel better but the following day, he was very curt with me. He was accusing me of being selfish and I didn't understand why. I really liked him so much already and given how desperate I was with my family situation; I was really hanging on to the possibility of him. But later that afternoon, his mood changed. He asked me again if we can hear mass together again. This time to a different church. That night, I had a feeling that something might happen between the two of us. We didn't exchange any romantic conversation because we were just getting to know each other but somehow, I knew, something is going to happen. It was so timely that it was on a Thursday – there was holy hour. I asked the Lord, "please guide me in my decisions. If he is the one you chose for me and something happens between the two of us tonight, I promise I will love him until the end of my life". It was like I was making a vow of marriage ahead thinking that making such vow will reduce the offense of sleeping with him outside of marriage.

True enough, when I went to drop him off, something indeed happened that I initiated, and as he asked me to spend the night with him, I hesitated. I prayed to God to give me wisdom. I really prayed. So, I told him and said, can we do this next time? But he said, "I don't think there will be a next time". It's important to note that I have been celibate for 14 years and I was already 40 years old. I was desperate with my entire family situation and I was not ready to let go of this momentary relief. I needed the companionship, more than I needed to breathe. So, I agreed. He was going to be the 3rd person I was going to be intimate with in all of my life. I was not expecting a lot. I just needed that moment. The following morning, I went home and he wanted me to stay. But I couldn't because I have a helper situation in my condo, with my many dogs. I didn't even text him afterwards. But what is different in my previous intimacy was that, this time, I didn't cry. I didn't feel bad. I didn't feel like something was wrong. I was totally fine. I was even confident. I didn't feel insecure at all. Quite the contrary, I felt secure. I was not bothered at all of anything. I was not even paranoid of possibly being used. I was just really chill.

The following morning, he messaged me again and asked me why I didn't tell him I got home. He later asked me if I want to go hear mass with him and I did, again. When I saw him walking in the street, as he loved doing – I initially felt turned off. In normal days, I really would not go out with someone like him but then, I remembered what happened the night before. And I remembered, this is my opportunity to give something a chance. Even if it will not turn out the way I expected, but I will do my best to learn from this relationship if it's ever going to go somewhere. Every night, I sleep with him and every day we heard mass. One time, while we were walking down the aisle, he said to me, let's practice walking down the aisle April. And I really wasn't thinking of marriage at all so I didn't get what he was talking about. But overtime, the idea continued to develop in my mind. He was the one who suggested the idea of marriage in my mind. We were receiving Holy Communion the entire time. I wasn't aware of the desecration we have been doing to the Holy Eucharist. I prided myself into thinking that God understands. Finally, I was able to settle my helper situation and I was able to stay the night with him. This was literally my first time to wake up in a man's house in all of my life. He woke me up with coffee, and very cool music. My feelings for him grew even more intense. He made me breakfast.

When we go to church, he would take my hand after mass and put it in his forehead. I didn't understand why he would do that but he would keep on doing that almost every after mass. There were so many things I didn't understand or have never tried at all.

But what was striking in all these was, it was effortless for me. For the first time in my life, I am just the passenger. It was as easy as my first boyfriend. He was leading the way the entire time and I was contented. After two weeks of being with him literally every night, I suddenly wondered if he had a girlfriend. It finally occurred to me to wonder. I totally panicked because I was already falling in love with him and I was just asking questions that I should have asked way early than a month ago – like before we even started. It was like I walked into a trance and I wasn't aware where I have been. I asked him if he had a girlfriend because I can see a lot of one female name in his house and I started to wonder if he was living with someone and I was the other woman. His answer was? No answer. He was the type who didn't like to be asked anything. He was the type who didn't like to be probed. Because he refused to answer, I decided to leave for Dumaguete with another diving friend. He started calling me incessantly. I asked him again if he had a girlfriend. He still wouldn't answer. But he would keep on messaging me as if I never asked him anything. He would keep on updating me what he was doing and he would ask me what I was doing. He would send me photos and all. So finally, I came home two or three days after. I demanded from him to tell me the truth. Then he said, he will only tell me if I talk to him in person. It will never be thru text or over the phone.

So, I went over to see him. He opened his statement with me so arrogantly, but said in a calm voice that he normally doesn't respond to demands. It's either I accept what he was willing to offer or that's it. And I said, I am not willing to continue seeing him unless he was upfront with me on the truth. He realized I was serious and I was ready to leave. So, he phrased his words very carefully. He said, somewhere along the line that goes, "I didn't tell you because I don't need to explain myself to you but since you asked, no, I don't have a girlfriend anymore" and told me they broke up a while back. I asked him if he was still in love with her, and he said, No. Then he said if I was going to ask any further, he will finally let me go. I suddenly got cold feet. I started wondering what we are to each other. I talked to him and said, I am getting scared. Maybe we should stop already. It may be better if we stop now before we go any deeper and it will be more painful to let go. He told me we can slow down. As slow as I want it to be. We were doing the same routine for the entire month. There was a time we fought again because maybe he was also married. He then told me what proof do I need or does he have to give me a Certificate of No Marriage (CENOMAR) and I said yes! He got mad why I don't just take his word for it. And I told him, that's how mistresses become mistresses because they took a man's word simply as it is. I told him, I know how it feels to be on the other side. It was never my dream to be anyone's mistress and he shouldn't be criticizing me for making certain I am not. He told me how he appreciated my values. He ended up giving me a CENOMAR.

Never at any point in that entire month was I made aware by the Holy Spirit of what we were doing - I had cold feet; I wondered if he had a girlfriend; but I completely forgot about Monsignor Krekeinbek. I completely forgot about my consecration. I completely forgot about my family. All I could think of was him and diving. I even briefly forgot about my family problems. I didn't even think of my dogs.

Over the next few days, I got my memory back. I suddenly remembered Monsignor, my consecration, my vow! I couldn't believe how could have I forgotten?! I started to shake. I started to become aware of everything and I was afraid – afraid of what I have done. Right there and then, without warning, I decided to leave for Balamban, it's almost an hour drive from the City, to go to confession to a priest from *Mary's Little Children Community (MLCC)* – it was also the time, I met my good friend, a religious sister.

I left him without warning and texted him that I am going to confession in Balamban, because I promised a friend I will accompany her. It is important to emphasize that I am normally a high-strung person and quite arrogant but the entire time I was with him, I have been significantly humbled. I have put a hold on my temper. I have grown significantly kind even to my father's workers. To my own helpers. I have become kind, patient and understanding.

So, when I went to confession, and described to the priest what I have been doing, it was me who told the priest that I think the enemy may have succeeded in hi-jacking me. Then the priest agreed with me. He said if I wanted to keep on seeing this guy, we have to get married. And I said, "but father, we are barely two months in! We cannot possibly get married already?" but father said, there is no other way because God will never permit this. I remember confessing to different priests and got the same response. Though some said it is something we can lift up to God's mercy but emphasis on marriage was very firm.

I was crying on my way home because I knew what I have to do. Fortunately, I was with my nun friend who has been comforting me the entire time. He was already texting me earlier that day. He wanted to hear mass with me but I said I will be home really late. He told me if he can still see me as soon as I get home, no matter how late. I said I will let him know. But I came home close to morning so it really didn't make sense to wake him up. I just messaged him.

Then the following morning, he asked me if we can hear mass together again. After mass, we went to his home and I had to tell him what I had to do. I explained to him about my spirituality. I told him about Monsignor. I told him how important my faith was. He got so mad at me. He said, I duped him – that I made him believe I was cool and now, all of a sudden, I am "super" religious. I told him, I still want to keep on seeing him if its okay with him that we won't be intimate. He just got mad. I thought it was over. I left and cried my heart out. Then he messaged me again after lunch and said he wanted to see me. I told him I thought we were over. He said, he just needed time to process what I told him. That night, he told me to sleep in his house. He promised, we won't do anything that will offend God. We will just sleep. I agreed and decided to trust him. True enough, it's exactly what we just did. I always treated sleeping in his house as "extended" overnights. I never really thought more of it than extended overnights.

We met in another church to hear mass, and he pointed on the list of marriage requirements again and he would say, take note of that and prepare your documents. I would look at him like "what are you talking about"? He would smile as if he didn't ask something that would confuse me.

That day, we fought. It started with him joking about asking me to prepare my marriage documents. But when we got around to talking about what our relationship was, he was being vague about it. He said, we don't need to label it. That started to concern me – the inconsistency. I told him maybe it's time to call it quits before we go any further. Each time we have that conversation, he would often sound like he agrees. We would part ways, then he would message me again as if we never had that conversation.

I was already ready to let him go when all of a sudden, he asked me to have lunch with his family. I have never been invited by a man to have lunch with his family. I wanted to try how it felt. So, I did. I thought there was going to be a lot of people, other than his family. I thought there was an event or gathering. But I was surprised to realize that it was literally just his family. He was feeding me so casually and serving me, in front of his family. I felt so welcomed. I felt like I belonged for the first time in my life. I felt like I was home. I have never tried that feeling before. I have never tried feeling like I belong to a family.

I was growing more confused. Then all of a sudden, he invited me to travel abroad with him and his friends, with his female best friend too. I was excited because I will finally be able to meet his best friend. I knew that they go a long way together, and I was ready to put my best foot forward so his best friend will like me also. It was just to my surprise that, somewhere along the way in that short trip, he stopped being sweet with me. It became even worse when his best friend along with all of his circle of friends from Hong Kong all came to Cebu. I was suddenly on the backseat. I suddenly became unimportant. I was so hurt because I have already grown so attached to him. As much as I want it over, but he wouldn't let me go and I simply cannot resist him. As far as I can remember, even during Christmas, I told him that we should put an end date to our being together so that I can prepare for it. He said, "forever". I asked him if he ever had plans of getting married, and he was always vague about it. He didn't want to talk about firm things. He invited me to have lunch with his family on Christmas day. It was so significant because I didn't have that with my own family. Although I gave my mom a Christmas present but we weren't really able to spend a proper Christmas together.

But as the days went by, I was further moved to the back seat. I was always upfront with him on everything. The same thing, he refuses to let me go. I still cannot stop myself from going back.

It was so timely that my old high school friend started to reach out to me again – and I decided to go back to Monsignor Kreikenbeek . I told him about what happened since the last time he saw me. I thought he would understand and would assure me things will be okay. Monsignor was always understanding with my friend's situation, which practically was much worse than mine. But Monsignor's reaction was so unexpected. He was very disappointed. He told me I have to stop seeing this guy. I told Monsignor that we go to church every day. And Monsignor said, it doesn't mean anything. He is using the mass so he can keep you within God's permissive will. And I said, isn't that a good thing Monsignor? And that's when I learned about two kinds of will. Permissive vs. Objective Will. Objective will lead to heaven whereas permissive leads to hell. Objective will require obedience to God, while permissive will is disobedience to God. Monsignor told me to consecrate myself to Mama Mary for three (3) months where it works like a retreat. It will be total silence. I won't talk to anyone. I agreed. I was preparing myself to sign a document for Monsignor to affix his signature as my Spiritual Director. I left a very long note to the man I was seeing, gave him two of my Exorcism books from Fr. Syquia, emphasizing his refusal to get married and what I am about to do with this consecration. I actually tricked him into meeting me on the other entrance, while I entered his house from the back entrance so I can leave him my long note and the exorcism books. I told monsignor what I did and he laughed. He asked me why I did that. And he just answered his question, he said, "because you love him". I said, yes Monsignor. I love him very much and I really want him saved. I negotiated with Monsignor if I can reduce the number of days from 3 months to one week only.

On the day of my consecration, the man I was seeing was there. I told him if he wants to talk to me, he has to ask Monsignor's approval. I asked him if he wants to confess to Monsignor but he refused.

Since that day, we stopped talking. He didn't message me. That was the first time since we started that we didn't communicate in one day. We would still see each other in the church, but we won't talk. He would leave a candle on my vehicle every day. Until the week was finally over. I finally called him. He answered me immediately. He got mad at what I put him thru yet despite that, he still picked up my call. I talked to Monsignor again that I cannot let him go and for the first time, the frail and sweet Monsignor, stomped his hand on the table. He was angry. He said, God was angry. I told Monsignor, I love him and I want him saved. And that was when Monsignor said to me, "do you think you can love him more than God? Of course, God loves him! More than you ever can! That's why you have to let him go. This is not love. This is obsession!"

I felt so hurt and I left. My old high school classmate was there and he asked Monsignor what will happen to me, Monsignor said, "She completed her consecration. She will be fine. The Blessed Mother will take care of her."

After that, one thing led to another. The man I was seeing introduced me to his cousins, to his aunt, who even gave him her room so we can sleep over. And the man I was seeing was even the one who firmly said, we will just sleep. We won't do anything else but just sleep. And it was exactly what we just did. Sleep.

Then the pandemic happened. I was afraid I won't see him and so we both agreed I will stay in his house. I still didn't think we were living together because I had no concept of what living together was about. Up until he brought it up, I was not aware that was what we were doing.

During this time, he was training me how to be in a relationship with him. I just followed his lead. I never do housework at home but he was always upfront with me in telling me the things he doesn't like. So since then, I would make sure I clean his room, I fold his clothes. We would take turns making morning coffee for each other. He always prepares breakfast for me. For the first time in my life, I could finally imagine being married to someone. Not just someone – but to him. I wanted to be married to him more than anything. I wanted it so much it hurts. We lived together for about four months. I was so happy with him. It is important to note that in those four months of living together like husband and wife, our physical intimacy was less than a handful to a point that I started wondering if he wasn't interested in me anymore. It was only four months but I feel like were married for 20 years. I noticed, every so often, he would push me away. I always lose out to all of his friends. I was never chosen first when it came to his friends. One day, I bought grapes from my worker and delivered it to his house. I was wearing house clothes. I suddenly felt embarrassed. I am a professional – a Catholic woman, and I am living in another man's house who isn't my husband. I started to feel ashamed of myself. My self-esteem was dropping. We would fight over petty things. He would get mad over trivial things. Several times, I threatened to leave but he would always stop me from leaving. Until the 2nd to the last attempt – he didn't stop me but it was me who just couldn't do it. That was the beginning of the end. One early morning, I woke up so early so I can clean my dog's poop because it was always the source of our fight. It was him who asked me to bring some of my dogs, which are primarily "indoor dogs." Two of them were manageable. However, one of my dogs – a tiny, 6-year-old toy poodle at that time, which happened to be the smallest and the most adorable tend to poop anywhere. He couldn't tolerate it because his dogs were trained to only poop in a certain part of his compound. He would often get mad at me because my dogs were so undisciplined – except for New York, my miniature poodle that I often bring to church with me.

When I got back up, I was brushing my teeth when all of a sudden, he came running towards me. I thought he needed to pee. But the next thing he did was he hugged me very tight. He told me he dreamt that he lost me. I was speechless. I didn't expect that. Later that day, he picked a fight with me. He was anti-Ferdinand Marcos and he knew already how loyal I was to him. On the earliest period of our relationship, I was all too willing to stop seeing him because he hated Marcos so much but he called me out on how ridiculous I was for throwing our relationship away over Marcos. Of course, I chose him. When we fought one time, I recall even telling him – you are making me choose you over God! I was asking him to marry me because I was acutely aware that every day, we were living together gets me closer to hell. Not just me but him too. My nun friend suggested that maybe we can ask for nuptial blessings but none of the priests would do that – unless it's someone he knows personally. He initially agreed. But I told him he has to be the one to look. All that matters is we ask God's blessing and commit to love each other till death do us part. But then he said, he will only do it because I wanted it but he doesn't believe in marriage. That's when I finally gave up. I said to him – "what is the point of getting married if you don't believe in it? It's useless!" I already knew that I was fighting a losing battle. I knew that for as long as I stay with him – nothing is ever going to change for us. I have done everything. I have tried everything. We were together nine months. It's not a long time for couples living together but for me, it was way long overdue.

The final straw was when he was watching a video on YouTube about a woman promoting a polygamous relationship, and I heard him saying, "I agree, I agree." I looked at him and said, what do you mean you agree? Are you telling me something? He got mad and said, he watches what he wants to watch and I should just mind my own business. I was asking him to explain again if there is something he wants to tell me because I am a big girl, I can take it. He just left that morning and came back late in the evening. I packed all my things already because I wasn't sure how the conversation would go. I always packed my things because I have always been planning to leave. This time, he disrespected me while I was talking to him. He turned off the lights and left the room. He went to talk with one of his friends who was boarding in his house. While he left me in the dark, in his room.

I went down to my car and started loading my things. It was the middle of pandemic with a midnight curfew. It was nearing midnight already. When I went back to his room, he reminded me that it may not be safe to leave because of the curfew. And I told him angrily, "If I don't leave now, I will never leave!" – I accused him of many things in the heat of anger. I have decided already. Like I always say, once I am decided, it's decided.

On my way home, I was stopped at check point. The police were asking me where I came from. I said while crying, "I came from another house and now I am going home". Fortunately, the police seem to understand what was happening to me. He let me go thru and I went home.

Our break-up relationship was longer than our actual relationship. It took about two to three years before I can finally say it was over and we finally cut all communications with each other. I messaged him, apologized to him for all the unfair things I was accusing him of. I detailed everything to him – hoping that we can have closure sooner than usual. I didn't leave out a single detail. I also hoped at that time that I was pregnant. I was having severe bleeding yet I was still hoping I was pregnant. I wanted it so badly. Before I went to the OBGYN, I started imagining there was a baby in my womb. I wanted to believe it so much. When the doctor said there was no evidence of any fetus on my womb, I cried. Heavily. The doctor was comforting me to try again next time. I needed that baby to validate all that I had with him. I thought if I had a baby, it would have all been worth it. I recall telling him after that unless he had plans of marrying me, I will never ever go back to that kind of set up. I told him, I will never suffer for any man that is not my husband. Never again.

Truth be told, I enjoyed taking care of him. I enjoyed serving him. It made my life meaningful. I could imagine doing this for the rest of my life and I knew, this is the life I can imagine doing. It didn't turn me off at all. I was happy to serve him because I loved him so much. However, the moment I realized we didn't have an end game, suddenly, it all didn't make sense anymore. I started questioning my worth. I started doubting myself. All my insecurities were suddenly suffocating me. I started panicking – asking myself, how stupid have I been?

I finally understood why friends and women I know in the past couldn't leave their partners. I knew now why it was difficult. Because I was finally one of those women. I couldn't figure out how I could have allowed myself to be put into that situation. How? This was the question that haunted me. Although God has answered me several times, but in my moments of weakness, I keep on going back into asking these questions. Why did God allow that to happen to me?

When I decided to leave, there was a part of me that thought he will fight for me - that he will ask me to marry him. He did fight for me in a way that he won't stop communicating with me or finding ways to communicate with me but each and every time, he was still not willing to marry me. When I become soft with him, he would seem to want to get back at me for making him work so hard to communicate with me. I feel like he would blame me each time he makes an effort to communicate with me. I started to feel afraid that for every effort he makes to win me, he will make me pay for it double. He would seem very inconsistent. He would tell me he will marry me for as long as there was no pressure but then I would recall the many times we have had that conversation while we were together and that conversation always goes back in circles. It never goes anywhere. It would always trap me into hoping for something and yet it wouldn't happen. I know I couldn't do any better. I have given him the very best of me – the very best version of me that I am capable of giving at that time. He wasn't the very best version of himself, yet I accepted him. I was willing to be with him knowing all of his flaws. I was willing to suffer for him because I loved him so much. But he could not accept the person that I am. That was the most painful part of everything. The part where he didn't think I am good enough. He didn't say it exactly like that but he said it in a way that goes, "Good for you that you can imagine me as your husband. But how about me? Have you thought about my needs? What I want?"

He was a vocal person, but at the same time, not. He was vocal on things he doesn't want, of which marriage was one of those. He doesn't tell me why. He doesn't share with me his reasons why not so I can at least understand. He doesn't tell me what he wants in the relationship except to stay in the *gray* zone. He expects me to know what he wants. He expects me to settle on what he wants and be content with the uncertainty of it. No assurance. Nothing solid to build on but only the assumption or the promise that there might be. His demands were way more than what I am capable of meeting. He expects me to listen and pay attention to all he was saying like he does, and I have difficulty focusing because I had so many things to think about -my family, my business, my future – of which I was hoping it was going to be him. I needed something concrete to hold on to. I thought it was going to be him. I wanted it to be him so badly. I have chosen him. I chose him. And the painful part of it all is that – he wouldn't choose me.

The rejection was very painful for me to accept. I was rejected once again. On top of that rejection, my mom and my siblings went on full offensive with me. I was kicked out of my office; my brothers confiscated the truck I was maintaining, my dad's workers had nowhere to go. After the pandemic, my 2nd elder brother renovated our ground floor office into my parent's residence but I later understood what motivated him to do so, because making it into a residence, he thought it will void the indefinite lease agreement my dad sign for me so I can continue holding office there. But since the office address didn't actually have a house number, the lease agreement also applies to our 2nd building – so I decided to utilize our warehouse. It didn't have any electricity.

My mother was very fickle then. Sometimes she would permit me but when my brothers talk to her, she would recant it. It was very unpredictable for me every day. To make things worse, as I was struggling to make ends meet for our projects, suppliers and workers' salaries, my mother and siblings were dead set on not making me collect anything. My mother would even go as far as telling my clients that I was a thief – that I am not really part of the company; that I am scammer who is trying to swindle our family. Imagine how that impacts clients when my mother is telling them that? Fortunately, by God's grace, because it was me who closed those projects, and all my actions were supported by corresponding legal documents that show I do have authority, even ownership in the business, they weren't swayed. Some clients were told not to work with me because I didn't have any money – and that I will not be able to finish the project. There were some I lost. But there were some who decided to stick with me and we were able to bring their project to fruition.

To help divert my attention to this impending catastrophe, I decided to embark on a 100Km swim challenge that was supposedly completed in a four-month period but I only managed to complete in less than three months. Then during the culmination, our last swim to complete the 100km mark, I gathered a few open water swimmers, organized an event in collaboration with Stand-Up Paddle, and Scuba Divers, as well as Free Divers, to go on an ocean cleanup activity while we cross the Olango Channel from Marigondon to San Vicente in Olango Island.

While it would seem that I was smiling but deep inside I was hurting so much. My pain became my motivation to complete such a challenge. It was only good for less than a year. I was really hoping that at the end of that year, I will grow more confident of my decision. The only difference this time compared to my past was that, I really gave all of me. In the past, it took me a while to get over because I always hesitated. I never allowed myself to be completely vulnerable. But this time, I did. I gave all of me and it was difficult to reconcile that in spite of giving all of me, I still fell short. It was different before when I was the sole judge of who I am.

It was harder to recover when someone you love with all of your heart rejected you for who you are. It was really painful to be rejected for who we are. I didn't even recover yet at that time from my own mother's rejection, and here comes a man whom I loved with all of I am, even choosing him over God despite the chances God has been giving me and yet, he still rejected me.

But did you know there is a reversal to this particular thought process? This vulnerability is also a gift because it allows one to learn about the virtue of humility. This vulnerability is a grace because it allows one to learn how to understand and be patient of the other. This vulnerability is a privilege because not everyone is given the opportunity to experience love in this manner.

Remember when I said that what matters when we die are not what we received but what we have given. When we are in the position that we are hurt because we loved – that, in and of itself is the greatest reward of all.

Pride was making it harder. Pride really knows where to hit me most. Naturally, pride blinds us from seeing the truth that will cause us to start second guessing our decisions. The good thing that was firm was my knowledge that there was nothing more that I can do. I have no control over his decision to love or accept me. But if we rest on this notion on "rejection" or not being chosen, 100% it will really keep on hurting us. When in truth, the person's rejection of us has nothing to do with us.

Our spiritual enemy truly know where to hit us the most if we are not careful. It will speculate on a memory that are still sensitive to us, and they will pounce on it. In fact, while I was writing above, I realized that I have not fully healed until I visited the Blessed Sacrament – and I spoke to the Lord, what can I truly do to overcome this. I already knew the answer except that, it is sometimes fleeting if we have not fully embraced the essence of the virtue.

There is actually a step-by-step process. When we think of rejection, we have to listen to the Holy Spirit when we examine if we have also rejected God? But what did God do with our rejection? Did he get mad? Did he abandon us? No. He gave us freedom to decide when we will call on him. I was also reminded on that moment when Monsignor asked me why I gave him my exorcism books, I was reminded because I love him and I cared for his soul. That is a sacred kind of love. When we think of the sanctity of love – the pain of rejection will cease to matter. The pain of not being chosen will cease to matter because true love will only care about what benefits one's soul.

Because true love, will make us accept the person and all their flaws. True love allows us to acknowledge the reality that our presence in their lives is not making them better and because we love them, we realize the necessity to let them go instead, so they will continue to grow in the direction they are supposed to – separate from us.

I kept asking the Lord that for the most part of my attempt to meet someone in the past, there were many things he didn't allow, but why did he allow this? And now that I have finally been anointed and spiritually cleansed, will God, all the more, allow me to do this to him? I kept asking what for?

Out of nowhere, an old Dutch friend of mine from I-House, whom I haven't seen in 15 years at that time, suddenly called me on my messenger. She is actually a Clinical Psychiatrist. We weren't really close but I remember her to be really nice but she wasn't the type you can actually be familiar with. I suddenly wondered why she called me up. I decided to pick up as I thought it was a mistake. She then said, "April? How are you? I am sorry I called you." At that time, I would welcome anyone who would call me. Anyone. She proceeded to telling me, "I know you may find this strange and you know I am a psychiatrist, right? And this may sound crazy but, when I was in I-House, I was baptized a Christian in Norwegian Baptist Church. Since my baptism, I have been receiving messages from God. I am calling you now to tell you that God said, you made the right decision. God said he is very happy with your decision." She said, whatever that is. God said it was right. I didn't tell her about the name of the person or that if it refers to the guy but she suddenly mentioned about "the guy".

I wanted to believe her but of course, I took her messages with caution. My religious sister friend was also a mystic but she also came from an ancestral background that practiced occultism. She helped me balance my Dutch friend's messages from God. During that time, these two were my support system. My Dutch friend would only call me when God has a message for me that she needs to deliver, but other than that, I cannot call her. I tried to but she will not pick up. When I get hit with severe anxiety remembering my previous relationship and I would beg the Lord to speak to me, my phone would ring and it would be her. Of course, she would always end her message telling me I need to confirm everything with God. Eventually, even though she wasn't Catholic, her messages to me significantly comforted me especially when dealing with my family problems. Her timing was always spot on. Especially when it came to making decisions where I would need my father to sign some documents, she would tell me to wait – to hold it. And then one day, she would call me all of a sudden and tell me, it's time. Even with what happened to my mother, she suddenly called me to tell me I have to start talking to my mom soon because something is going to happen to her. She kept telling me to do so ASAP. And so, I did. It was so fortunate when I did because I was able to respond to my mom's health scare precisely because I already reached out to her. If I didn't, the caregiver wouldn't have informed me. She would also tell me to tell my mom everything that I went thru – she said I must. And I did – which significantly helped in repairing my relationship with my mom. She was like a coach who kept assuring me that my purification process is almost over – that God told her, everything will be just fine. She described to me that when a person is healing, the healing process is the most painful. And each time I felt I could not bear it any longer, she would call me again and say, God said to hang in there and that I am almost there. True enough, the storm finally passed. After about three years or so. The worst storm of my life has finally passed. This is not to say that there were no more storms after this but there were many more, much worse, but I have already developed the spiritual muscles to endure it.

I truly believed that though she had a double antenna (meaning, I believe she can hear God's message but she can also hear the enemy). I just learned to sift thru her messages to me but what kept me protected was, over the course of our communication – I felt compelled to hear mass daily, and had been a daily communicant since 2021.

My being a daily communicant significantly helped in my healing, which lead to where I am now in spirituality. Then one day, I started to hear God's answer, in the back of my head – through images – telepathic, similar to what I experienced in Vietnam. God's answer couldn't be clearer than clear. I am so used to the pain caused by my family. Offering their pain to God doesn't mean I have truly sacrificed something because I didn't really have much of a choice but to surrender it to God.

I don't really have anything so huge to offer to God until this opportunity of loving this man came. I could have chosen to stay with him – choose him over God. He was willing to stay with me for as long as we don't get married – or who knows until when? But the bottom line was, the reason why I left him was because I want to stop offending God.

This makes the perfect offering to God because God knows how much I love him and I was willing to give him up for my fear and love of God. And I asked again, *"why did I have to love him this much? I wouldn't have known what I am missing Lord. Why do I have to learn of this kind of love?"*

Then the Lord gently answered, ***"so you will recognize how you have fallen in love with me."*** God always uses human beings to teach us to love- such kind of love can only come from God.

In Love with God

When I was still deciding on the title of this book, I wondered if I should say, "An atheist's guide to finding God" but even if logically, it makes more sense but spiritually, it doesn't. It isn't enough to find God. Finding God is just the initial step. Falling in love is the true manifestation that we have truly found God because we are able to perceive God's language of love.

Love for God is fundamental in knowing God. It will not be possible to know God, to know Jesus, or to understand humanity without love. Love for God, Love for Jesus and Love for humanity is fundamental in knowing the truth. Love is vital. I truly pray for the whole world to fall in love with God so the world will truly know him.

I stopped caring about what other people think but more on what God thinks of my thoughts and decisions, and it gets really hard because I still walk the earth and, in most times, my hands are tied that I'd find myself deciding which one is the lesser evil. The degree of difficulty increases the more I progress in faith. It really doesn't get any easier. But love is indeed powerful. Very powerful.

When I fell in love with a "person", it was powerful enough to make me *"change"* my ways. But when I fell in love with God, it is powerful enough to *"sustain"* the change. This is not to say I don't get mad; I still do. I just don't dwell on it any more than I used to. It's so much easier now to forgive and move on yet it gets harder for me to be tolerant of those who refuse to believe and value God. I can understand now why it is easier for people to label religious people as bigots. If one would think, when we fall in love with a person, no matter what other people think of that person we won't listen because the love we feel is so powerful. We would get hurt if people demonize or criticize the person we love. We would want to avoid those people and cut them off.

The hard part of falling in love with God is, by being in love with God means we also must love his creation – all of his creation no matter how unlovable they are. So even if there are people who hate or deny God, I know God will *not* be happy if I cut them off. It is so difficult. I can easily forgive people who hurt me now but I am not yet as tolerant to accept those who hurt God or deny him. Again, it is very difficult. I really don't know how to do it. What I do is just pray for them or offer masses. Or pretend I didn't hear them but pretending is also a form of dishonesty that is inconsistent with Christ's ways. The intolerance remains. It's quite a struggle. Pride does come in many forms.

Humility is one virtue that is really so painful to acquire. How can we demonstrate true obedience to God, thru the authority of the Catholic Church without the clergy? The Catholic Church was created by God, founded by Jesus Christ himself, the only church written and mentioned in the bible; it isn't just a mere religion or a political construct. It is our home – a universal home or a ship established by God to take us (all of humanity) safely to his kingdom.

It isn't enough that we are baptized Catholic if we don't imitate Jesus. It isn't enough that we are baptized Catholic if we allow other people to be separated from God when we are placed in a position to speak the truth, no matter how uncomfortable and inconvenient and if we continually refuse to fulfill our obligation. Our job as Catholics is to keep speaking the truth no matter how it is received for in that truth, the Holy Spirit will do the rest. The important thing is, we spoke the truth. Catholics need to realize our responsibilities because we are Christians. It is for every Catholic to step up and stand by the truth (not the religion) – the truth of God's ultimate goodness. It is for every Catholic to live like Christ and strive to save every brother that are away from God.

It is for every Catholic to take arms and engage in battle against enemies who are demons (demons are spiritual beings, and don't have any flesh) NOT people, thru ardent prayers; firm resolve to transform into the Christian values demonstrated by Jesus from Birth to Death so that we can bring all of humanity, as <u>One</u>, under God's kingdom. Being Catholic is a responsibility. It is a religion of the cross – our job is to suffer for those who refuse to be saved. Our job is to suffer so people can transform. Our job is to sacrifice so people can learn to love God, and ultimately love all of humanity.

Being Catholic is not a birthright – it is a choice and a responsibility. Being baptized Catholic as a baby is a privilege given by God – "Do Not Waste It!" It's a privilege so you can suffer for the salvation of mankind and share in Christ's suffering.

It's a privilege to be given that task and understand the task because our existence has a purpose. It is a privilege because others go thru life lost, unaccounted for, proud and caged by the choices of their ancestors, which we really don't have any control over. We can only pray for them and by divine grace, we hope that the Holy Spirit will successfully pierce thru the deceptions of the evil one, which has held many of these souls' captive for centuries since time immemorial.

But by God's grace, we have control over our CHOICE to be steadfast with our love for God; our CHOICE to be vigilant that we are not deceived; and our CHOICE to persevere in loving those away from God. My words don't reflect the usual language of catechism. I have long forgotten what I learned since grade school. The words that I find myself using is from my direct experience of faith thru my love of God. Though my words are unorthodox but the tenor and essence of it are validated in the Catholic doctrine. I can only speak from my heart based on what has been revealed to me. So, pardon me for sounding certain.

There's another side to the struggle and challenges that makes "life interesting and less boring" and it is on how to deal or handle harmony and peace. Can one be content with it? Monetary success doesn't last forever. People can get sick. People can have one awful encounter that can change a lifetime of success. Having a family is a calling. Some people are called to have one. Some are called to do something else. Just be who you are in all its goodness.

In most times, we struggle to keep the peace but for people who came from abusive and traumatic environments, often times struggle on being content with a peaceful life that we inadvertently look for trouble without fully realizing it. I learned that psychological healing is as equally important in spiritual healing, which means that the science of Psychology, Anthropology and Sociology (understanding people and society) are also critical in spiritual healing.

How do saints maintain to stay in Christ's state of grace in spite of all the troubles in the world? The devil is allowed to exist for a specific reason, to test us. It was never God who is testing us. It's the devil. Because God created us in his own image and likeness, he gave us freewill. He is a jealous God precisely because he wants us to *choose* him consciously and not him commanding us to choose him.

And the answer I got is to Love God above all else. When we truly *love* him, we can endure all pain. When we truly love him, we are confident despite our losses. When we truly love God, we can forgive all the people that hurt us including ourselves because no one is greater than God but God alone. This is our overarching goal. To be able to get here, God gave us the tools using knowledge thru arts and science to get there; granting we never lose sight of God and our spirituality. Everything must be centered on God and God alone.

As the unbelievers would claim that how can a good God allow or permit such violence and trials to a person if he isn't an evil God? But the alternative to that is, if we follow Christ, where we:

> HUMBLE ourselves to the knowledge that we are only a creature,
> FORGIVE our oppressors,
> LOVE our enemies;

What does an evil God gain with all those virtues he wants us to live by? How can a humble heart lead to conflict? How does forgiveness lead to chaos? And how does love lead to cruelty?

Faith in God is not as simple as simply "believing" without working on ourselves or dealing with our inner traumas and finding the courage to heal ourselves. Merely relying on psychology without the "belief or faith in God" is not sustainable as well. Humility, forgiveness and love can be faked but it cannot be "fathomable" because it is only thru God's grace that we can fathom humility, forgiveness and love. The key to salvation is hard work! Hard work to reform, transform and do penance. Hard work to sacrifice for the salvation of not just the self but of those who refuse to believe. If we, Christians, fail to do our part and do the best we can to bring those who are far away closer to God and they fail? It's our failure too, not just theirs.

We cannot say, it's "their choice" if we haven't done our part or sacrificed enough to a point that we allow ourselves to be ridiculed. We have to exhaust everything we've got to emphasize the truth for their salvation too. Our salvation is largely dependent on our efforts to help bring those who are far away closer to God. We only need to help the Holy Spirit to penetrate a doubter and consider for a slight millisecond to let God's love work thru him. It is so frustrating to see fellow Christians resting in their illusions that just because they are baptized and not offer sacrifices think their path to salvation is secured.

Ultimately the definition is the willingness to "suffer and take up one's cross with gratitude". Imitating Jesus Christ is simply the willingness to suffer and sacrifice for the love of God, which translates to finding courage to love people we hate, we abhor or people that repulse us because we love God more. And I admit, it's so hard to do. Super hard. Alternatively, self-control is equally as important. Mercy and generosity can also have its own perilous outcome and can also be hijacked by the enemy. Self-control is critical to discern God's will. Too much mercy and generosity could aid in a person's lack of remorse or accountability. We have to be careful that when we give mercy, compassion and generosity that it will lead to reform not reinforce bad behaviors.

Sometime in 2022 – my mother almost died and at that moment, I was the one given the position to decide if she will be intubated or not. It was a difficult decision for me because if I agreed and she died, I know my siblings will feast on me. But by the grace of the Holy Spirit, I made the right decision. I begged the Lord for mercy.

In gratitude to God's mercy, I was the one who reached out to my brother, as commanded by my mother to ask for his forgiveness – for us to have peace. It was the beginning of my reconciliation with my mother that led to her gradual liberation. We still have a long way to go but at least, we are going somewhere. Only God knows when he will lift the suffering because our suffering, when it makes us weak also makes us very strong. Because in that weakness, we learn to be humble. When we are humble, we are undefeatable.

Be grateful for every suffering you experience because every pain, sorrow and misery are an opportunity to share in Christ's suffering. If one has that awareness, one can *SAVE SO MANY SOULS*, not just our own. It is so tempting to be comfortable and live comfortably. Especially me – I love to sleep and just laze around but that's not going to help my soul. Zero benefit at all. Quite the contrary. I have reached a point in my life where my relationship with the Almighty is enough to stop me from contemplating revenge. I still get irritated, impatient and upset with people who wronged me but it doesn't stick for long. I am more concerned of embarrassing God that lately, I find myself crying more often (out of anger) instead of lashing out. I get embarrassed by feelings of bitterness because I know God can see my thoughts.

I understand the full implication of sharing my entire life story in a book and this is my ultimate sacrifice. To expose my life and my soul for my love of God – for what is the point of my life if I cannot share it in order to demonstrate being a witness to God's love? For those who loves God, please pray for me that I may endure what may happen next. Please pray for me that no matter what happens, God will not allow me to be separated from him.

www.ingramcontent.com/pod-product-compliance
Lightning Source LLC
Chambersburg PA
CBHW011228120626
46549CB00008B/3187